Edward Tanjore Corwin

Historical Discourse

on occasion of the centennial anniversary of the Reformed Dutch church

of Millstone - Vol. 1

Edward Tanjore Corwin

Historical Discourse
on occasion of the centennial anniversary of the Reformed Dutch church of Millstone - Vol. 1

ISBN/EAN: 9783337302795

Printed in Europe, USA, Canada, Australia, Japan

Cover: Foto ©Andreas Hilbeck / pixelio.de

More available books at **www.hansebooks.com**

HISTORICAL DISCOURSE

ON OCCASION

OF THE

CENTENNIAL ANNIVERSARY

OF THE

Reformed Dutch Church,

OF

MILLSTONE.

BY

EDWARD TANJORE CORWIN, PASTOR.

1866.

NEW-YORK:

J. J. REED, PRINTER, 43 CENTRE STREET.

1866.

THE
Early Purchasers
of
HILLSBOROUGH AND
FRANKLIN TOWNSHIPS.
SOMERSET CY. N. J.
Compiled from Reeds Map 1685,
and local Maps.

PREFACE.

The Reformed Dutch Church of Hillsborough, at Millstone, celebrated her centennial anniversary on Saturday, August 11th, 1866. The following Historical Discourse was delivered by the pastor, on the morning of that day, in connection with appropriate religious exercises. On motion of Hon. A. O. Zabriskie, its publication was called for, with the request that notes and appendices be added. The writer has accordingly given it to the public, hoping that thereby, the memory of early times may be preserved, and also, (which is more important,) that by a proper appreciation of the past, Israel may understand what she ought to do in the future.

Having noticed shortly after his settlement at Millstone, that the church was rapidly completing her first century, he directed his attention, as time permitted, to her history, and in the course of a couple of years, the within material collected in his hands. The sources whence he has gathered his facts, were the Millstone Church Records, (which are complete, with the exception of four years, 1810–1814,) and the records of some of the neighboring churches ; the minutes of Classis, and of the early Synod, and such local histories and biographical notices as could be found ; the Documentary and Colonial Histories of New York ; the early Colonial Records at Amboy and Trenton, and some few private papers. He also feels particularly indebted to the "Contributions to the History of East Jersey," and other volumes, of Wm. A. Whitehead, Esq., which have proved of great value, both in facts given, and in directing to sources of information. Hon. Ralph Voorhees, of Middlebush, loaned a number of papers, from which the facts concerning the church at Three Mile Run were gleaned, and for which the writer would express his thanks ; and also especially indebted is he to Mrs. E. F. L. Read, and Miss Sarah C. Souder, of Philadelphia, for their kind and valuable assistance in reference to the pastorate of Rev. Mr. Foering, the first regularly installed minister in this place. He would also take this opportunity of returning his thanks to Rev. Mr. Kiekenveldt and Mr. Louis H. Bahler, for valuable assistance in the translation of Dutch and German documents.

MILLSTONE, *August* 30*th,* 1866.

Millstone Centennial Anniversary.

August 11, 1866.

The following was the Programme of the occasion :—

Chant—(Ps. 90)—by the **Choir.**

Invocation :
By REV. W. J. R. TAYLOR, D.D.

Reading of Scriptures—(Ps. 103):
By REV. C. C. VAN CLEEF.

Prayer :
By PROF. DE WITT, D.D.

Singing—Hymn **458.**

Historical **Discourse**
By the Pastor.

Singing—Ps. 137, 3d Part..........Benediction.

RECESS.

Singing—Ps. 87.

ADDRESS BY REV. GABRIEL LUDLOW, D.D.
(Reminiscences of Drs. Cannon and Schureman.)

ADDRESS BY REV. P. D. VAN CLEEF, D.D.
" " REV. J. C. SEARS, D.D.
" " HON. A. O. ZABRISKIE.
" " HON. F. T. FRELINGHUYSEN.
" " PROF. JOHN DE WITT, D.D.

Anthem by the **Choir.**
Doxology..........,.................Benediction.

PRESENT CHURCH OFFICERS.

PASTOR:
EDWARD TANJORE CORWIN.

ELDERS:

RALPH TERHUNE SUTPHEN,   JAMES LONGSTREET VOORHEES,

ROELOFF DITMARS,   JOHN SMITH.

DEACONS:

JOHN VREDENBURGH VAN NEST,   CORNELIUS HOAGLAND BROACH,

FREDERICK T. SMITH,   JOHN STAATS.

HISTORICAL DISCOURSE.

THE histories of the individual churches of Christ are worthy of preservation, because they represent the efforts of particular communities, to carry forward, at least in their own localities, those glorious principles of heavenly truth, which the Saviour brought from heaven, and which when understood and appropriated, will regenerate mankind. Each faithful church stands as the representative of the kingdom of Heaven, of the triumphs of righteousness, on the earth. Her history must therefore ever be the record of noble deeds of piety and love; of steady, earnest effort in the work of enlightening, benefiting, and saving men; of pure devotedness to the Spirit and cause of the Master. It is true, indeed, that each church lives in an atmosphere of sin, that the imperfections of even the friends of Christ, tend often greatly to obscure her glory, so that in her efforts to build up the cause of truth and righteousness, the world may look upon her as a simple belligerent, having no superior aims to her opponents; nevertheless, each church is a little rill, helping to make up the ever-swelling tide of Christian influence, which is flowing onward with resistless volume, to purify and save our race. And if a church's history, as a whole, represent progress in this direction; if it show souls gathered into the kingdom; if a community have been leavened with Christian truths, or better still, with Christian practices, and been made to appreciate, and exhibit, the Eternal Law of Love—then has that church accomplished a great and glorious mission. She has performed her part, though imperfectly, in the grand manœuvres of that great army, whose Captain is Jesus Christ, and by which army, in all the harmony of the plan, which shall ultimately be developed even to our understandings, shall the world be conquered to the obedience of the faith.

It should, therefore, be a profitable task for us, as a church, at this marked period of our history, to glance over the past, that our memories may be refreshed, and our souls quickened anew, as we enter upon the second century of our career. For with each succeeding age, is the church of Christ called to higher duties and responsibilities, to greater self-denials and boldness in the cause of the Master—a proper understanding of which ever-expanding duties, it would be sad for her to fail to appreciate. But while dwelling upon and getting almost lost, perhaps, in interesting details, yet let us ever remember that the ultimate objects of history are, by understanding the Providence of God, to enable us to mount from the experience of the past to higher elevations in the future.

I am requested by the Consistory to give to-day, not only a history of the church, but also as necessarily introductory to it, a brief sketch of the civil settlement of this region. The civil history, before the period of our church, naturally divides itself into two parts. First, the Dutch sway, lasting from the first settlement of the country for a little more than half a century,* (1609–1666) ; and second, the English sway, lasting for a little more than a century, (1664–1776).

---

* The Synod of Dort (1618–19,) was held just before the time that the Dutch emigration fairly began. The Dutch West India Company, which gave great impetus to emigration, was chartered in 1621 ; the monopoly of the company was abolished in 1638.

During the Dutch sway, the central portions of New Jersey, including of course our own localities, remained entirely unsettled, and almost untrodden by the foot of a European.* The Dutch clung to the shores of the great rivers on either side of our State, and to the immediate vicinity of the noble harbor of the western world. † Perhaps the yet vivid remembrance of the encroaching seas of Holland, which they loved to fight so well, kept them so near the coast; perhaps their paucity of numbers, though they had reached 10,000 before the English conquest; perhaps the hostilities of the Indians, in the interior, with whom they had had some misunderstandings, though the natives of the soil, in all our State, only numbered 2,000 ; ‡ or perhaps their love of trade, and a mariner's life, or still other reasons, may have kept them along the shores of the larger bays and rivers. And although some grants of large tracts of land, covering portions of our county, § were

---

* Mr. Rockhill Robeson, now living at Weston, has informed me, since this was written, that private papers in his family state that his ancestry settled on the Millstone Branch of the Raritan in 1642, and in 1666 moved to Philadelphia.

† A few Dutch had penetrated and settled near Hackensack, as early as 1644.—*Whitehead's East Jersey, p.* 277.

‡ The Indians of New Jersey were divided among twenty petty kings, of whom the king of the Raritans was the greatest. About 1655 there was quite a slaughter by the Indians, around New Amsterdam, Pavonia, Staten Island, and Long Island. In 1640 the Raritan Indians had been wrongfully accused of theft, and a number of them killed.—*Riker, p.* 37.

The seat of the Raritan kings was upon an inland mountain (probably the Nechanic mountain, which answers approximately to the description).—*See Whitehead's E. J., p.* 24.

§ Augustine Herman received, in 1651, a square of land, having the Raritan from Amboy to North Branch for its southern side.—*Whitehead, pp.* 19, 37, 38.

made during the Dutch government of the country, yet not
a single Dutch settlement was made in the interior. *

The English, meanwhile, claimed the territory of the
New Netherlands by right of prior discovery, † but did not
make very strenuous efforts to conquer the Dutch, ‡ until
1664; and among other reasons or pretexts, one was that
the Dutch refused to allow the people of New England to
settle in the New Netherlands. The conquest was made
unexpectedly, and therefore easily, and a little more than
two centuries ago, the Dutch sway passed away from
America forever.

But with this change of government, the emigration from
Holland virtually ceased. The Dutch families in this
country (excepting the more recent immigrants), have all
been here, it may be safely said, for more than two centuries, or about seven generations. But with the English
conquest, a new period of colonization and settlement of
the territory of our present State began.

The English sway lasting for 112 years, divides itself into
three marked periods; viz., under Carteret, for eighteen
years, under the Proprietors for twenty, and the rest of the
time, seventy-two, under the crown. The New Netherlands
extended from the borders of Connecticut to the Delaware
River. But as the English fleet started on their mission of

---

* We of course except the remarkable Dutch settlement, long lost in
the wilderness, of Minisink, begun in 1634.—*See Gordon,* p. 10.

† Sebastian Cabot, in 1498, sailed along the coast.

‡ In 1634 England granted to Sir Edmund Ployden and his associates
all the lands between Long Island Sound and Cape May. This was
erected into a free county palatine, to be called New Albion, and it is
said he ruled over five hundred people. (?) He returned to England in
1741. The Dutch offered to sell out at one time, but not being
accepted, they finally refused to sell altogether.

conquest, so certain did Charles II., king of England, feel
of accomplishing it, that he gave the territory of the Dutch
to his brother James, Duke of York and Albany; and he in
turn, while the fleet was yet on the sea, to raise money for
his extravagances, ceded a large part of his newly acquired
territory west of the Hudson, that is, the territory of our
present State, to Sir George Carteret, and Lord John
Berkeley. Philip Carteret, a brother of Sir George, was
appointed governor, which position he held with slight in-
terruption* for eighteen years, (1664–1682,) and this is the
first period of the English sway.

During his administration, there was a large English immigration to this State, both from Old England and from
New. The policy of Carteret and Berkeley, was very liberal. They published and scattered their offers to settlers,
in what were called, "Grants and Concessions," which were
nothing else than a sort of republican constitution,† members elected by the people, forming part of the legislature ‡
and grants of 150 acres of land being given to every man,
and smaller quantities to women and to servants, after a
time, who would come and settle, provided the men and
servants could come armed with a musket and provision
for a few months. The population of the province was thus
vastly increased by English settlers, who located around

* In 1673 the Dutch re-conquered the State and held it for one year.
In 1679, Andross, governor of New York, made Carteret a prisoner for
a time, endeavoring to unite New Jersey to New York, but without
success.

† They contrasted it with that of Carolina, which was aristocratic.—
Whitehead's E. J. p. 308.

‡ The first legislative assembly was held in 1668, when Bergen, Elizabethtown, Newark, Woodbridge and Middletown, were represented.
These were at that time the only towns.

Amboy, Woodbridge, Elizabethtown and Newark. But
no settlements were made during this time up the Raritan,
or on its tributaries, although a few grants of land in this
county, on the north of the Raritan, were given.*

But during this time, Berkeley having failed, West Jersey was set off as his portion to be sold for the benefit of his
creditors, and East Jersey remained to Carteret. The first
division line soon after run, (1676,) is the present western
bound of our county, that is, south of the South Branch of
the Raritan. But Sir George Carteret, dying in 1679, East
Jersey, his property, was sold for the settling of his estate,
and after some legal manœuvering for three years, it finally
became, in 1682, the property of twelve proprietors, all
Quakers, with William Penn at the head.† Each of these
sold out one half of his interest to another person, so that
in this same year, East Jersey became the property of
twenty-four proprietors, embracing almost every religious
sect.‡ This was done from motives of policy.

---

*John Bailey, Daniel Denton, and Luke Watson, of Long Island, pur-
chased the tract formerly purchased by Augustine Herman, for articles
valued at $200. The same Indians sold the same tract, twice, (1651
and 1664.) It was bought by permission of Gov. Nicholls, not knowing
at the time of the cession already of New Jersey to Carteret and Berkeley. This was ultimately the cause of the great Elizabethtown bill in
chancery respecting the lands north of the Raritan, about a century ago,
and which, after many years of litigation, was dropped at the Revolution, and never revived.

† They paid £3,400 for East Jersey. Their names were : William
Penn, Robert West, Thomas Rudyard, Samuel Groom, Thomas Hart,
Richard Mew, Ambrose Riggs, John Haywood, Hugh Hartshorne,
Clement Plumstead, Thomas Cooper, and Thomas Wilcox, who at once
sold out his interest.

‡ The names of the additional purchasers, were. James, Earl of Perth,
John Drummond, Robert Barclay, (the first Governor), David Barclay,

These proprietors liberally governed their territory, and it is under them that the Raritan and Millstone valleys began to be settled. Their sway lasted, with some little interruptions, from 1682, for twenty years. Each of them had an equal interest in the territory, and either of them could have his share* set off to him in lands unappropriated, or could sell out his interest or a portion of his interest, or jointly, they could deed away any tract of land, which was generally done by a fully authorized agent. Within two years after East Jersey became the property of the proprietors, the South side of the Raritan, from below New Brunswick to Bound Brook,† was laid out in nineteen lots,‡ having in general, a little less than half a mile of river-front, and about two miles in depth, extending in this vicinity, to the neighborhood of Middlebush, and the most of these were in process of improvement. The last one of these lots having its face on the Raritan immediately below Bound Brook, followed the curve of that river, and extended back almost to the mouth of the Millstone, or to the present farm of Henry Garretson, and with the adjoining plot on the South, was owned by Mr. William Dockwra, the two containing 900 acres; and behind these, facing the Millstone, were a

Robert Gordon, Arent Sonmans, Gawen Lawrie, Edward Byllinge, James Braine, William Gibson, Thomas Barker, Robert Turner, and Thomas Warren.

* One share or propriety, contained 10,800 acres.

† John Inions & Co., bought on Nov. 1st, 1681, two lots, where now stands New Brunswick, containing a mile of river-front, and two miles of depth. In 1683, Middlesex was assessed £ 10 in a tax of £ 50, being one of the four counties then existing. In 1694, a *permanent* ferry was Established at New Brunswick.—*Whitehead's Amboy, p.* 269.

‡ See first map of East Jersey, made in 1685, which locates these lots. (*Library of Historical Society, Newark.*)

couple of lots reaching to the present farm of Benjamin
Smith, the lower, containing 800 acres, and belonging to
George Willox; and the upper, containing 500 acres and
belonging to Mr. William Dockwra, before mentioned. On
the north side of the Raritan,* from Bound Brook to the
North Branch, and extending back to the Blue Hills, as
they were called, six large plots† had already been survey-
ed and laid off to as many parties or companies; while the
large tract of land on the south, extending from the mouth
of the Millstone, three and a half miles up the Raritan, to
an island, just above the present covered bridge, and thence
running south by west, about two miles; and east, two
miles to the Millstone, on a line which is said to be the present northerly line of Mr. James Elmendorf's farm,‡ this
tract containing 3,000 acres, (exclusive of 250 acres of
meadows), § having been bought a few years before, by a
company consisting of Capt. Anthony Brockholls, William
Pinhorne, John Robinson, Capt. Mathias Nicholls, and
Samuel Edsall, was in the year 1685 confirmed to Royce &
Co., of New York, and to be thenceforward known by the
name of Royeefield.‖ So that the only lands taken up on

---

* In 1685 John Forbes took up about 400 acres of land on the Raritan,
about twenty miles above Amboy, for the purpose of improvement and
speculation.—See *Whitehead's E. J. p.* 321.

† Beginning at Bound Brook, the names of these owners were: Rudyard, Codrington, White,—Graham, Winder, & Co.—Robinson, and
Lord Neill Campbell.

‡ Peter G. Quick.

§ These meadows had been formerly granted to James Graham, John
White, Samuel Winder, and Cor. Courzen.—*Liber A.* 273, *Amboy Records.*

‖ The bounds were: beginning at a place called "Hunter's Wigwam"
on the Millstone River, thence north by west, two miles to a fresh
brook called Manamtaqua; thence north by east and north north-east,
to the Raritan River, opposite the west end of a small island, formerly

the Millstone in the year 1685, were these two plots near
its mouth, on the east side, owned by Willox and Dockwra,
(now called Weston,) and the one on the west side, owned
by Royce, excepting a little plot, at the mouth of Stony
Brook,* away up the stream solitary and alone in the wilderness, which had previously been purchased by Dr. Henry
Greenland. What a change in 180 years! Where all is
now smiling farms, interspersed with Christian temples,
then roamed the savage; and only seldom, and timorously
too, had civilized man ventured to break the stillness of the
scene, by his adventurous tread.

Within six years after the proprietors began to dispose of
the land, the population along the Raritan had so increased,†
that they had the new county of Somerset ‡ set off from

belonging to Robert Vanquellin, and now in possession of John Robinson; and thence down the Raritan three and a half miles; and up the
Millstone to the place of beginning.

* This can hardly be the Stony Brook, now known by that name, above
Princeton, but must be another stream near Rocky Hill, then called by
that name. Reed, on his map in 1685, locates him on Stony Brook,
but not above fourteen miles above the mouth of the Millstone.

† The great thoroughfares from Amboy and Brunswick to the Delaware were laid out about this time. In 1682, the population was about
4,000 (Smith, p. 161.) In 1689, it was estimated at 10,000.

‡ Bergen, Essex, Middlesex and Monmouth, the first counties, were
made in 1682, the eastern and northern bounds of Middlesex being then
about the same as now, and running westward to the limits of the province (which had not yet been fixed by survey). In 1687, the division
line between East and West Jersey was first run, and this became the
western bound of the new county of Somerset. But this line, the owners of West Jersey always insisted, bore too much to the west; therefore, in 1743, another line was run, which passed through the centre of
our present township of Hillsborough, being altogether east of Nechanic
Mountain, and of which the line between Stillwater and Newtown townships, in Sussex county, is still a vestige.—See *Gordon*, p. 73.

Middlesex, although it was not till some time after, that the
bounds of the new county were made to include the Valley
of the Millstone, * in this vicinity. But it was now a stir-
ring period of settlement and colonization. Glowing ap-
peals were made respecting the desirability of the lands on
the Raritan and its branches, and the large patentees had
hardly received their grants before they found many eager
purchasers for smaller tracts. On June 10th, 1688, Wm.
Dockwra, for having induced large emigration from England and Scotland to New Jersey, received patents for 2,000
acres in the valleys of the Millstone † and Raritan, and for
3,815 acres on the tributaries of the Millstone,—to be afterwards located. He also came into possession of many other
immense tracts of land, in various parts of the province.
He was a Scotchman by birth, but at this time a merchant
in London. The proprietors had such confidence in him,
that they gave him full powers of attorney to cede lands in
East Jersey at his own option. But, sad to say, he abused
their confidence, to his own interest, and was subsequently
superseded.‡ He died in 1717.§

* The present turnpike line, between Somerset and Middlesex, was
fixed in 1766.—*Early Records of New Brunswick, Map.*

† "The western part of Middlesex County is watered by *Millstone
River*, which runs through a pleasant valley belonging to Mr. William
Dockwra, of London."—*Extract from Oldmixon's Hist. Brit. Emp.,* fur-
nished by *Wm. A. Whitehead, Esq.*

These lands were mostly on the east side of the Millstone, extending
from the present farm of Mr. Cropsey, more than two miles up the
river. He also came into possession of 6,800 acres in Montgomery
township, north of Blawenburgh, in 1706, which he sold the next year
to John Van Horne.

‡ Governors Rudyard and Lawrie had acted a similar part, with
lands on the Raritan, and with a similar fate.

§ Mr. Dockwra was never in this country.

About 1690, Capt. Clement Plumstead obtained a large grant of land, including the territory of our present village. William Plumstead (probably a brother,) had lands to the north-west, in the vicinity of the farm of the late Henry Wilson. Clement Plumstead's land extended up the Millstone two miles, to what is now Blackwell's Mills, and west, to the road leading by the present John P. Staats' house to Cross Roads. Thomas Barker had the next plantation up the stream, having a mile and a half of river front, and extending west as far as Plumstead's; while Mr. Hart and Walter Benthall owned the next two plantations, which carry us up to the hills this side of Princeton.

The next large plot of land in this vicinity was purchased or inherited by Peter Sonmans.* His father, Arent Sonmans, was one of the twenty-four proprietors,† and who, at length, became possessed of five full shares of East Jersey. In 1693, his son Peter obtained a deed for about 36 square miles of the western part of our present township of Hillsborough, and a large part of Montgomery. His line began near Clover Hill,‡ and ran S. E. along the present county

---

* Mr. Sonmans was a native of Holland, having been educated at Leyden, and held important offices under the Prince of Orange, after he became King William III. He was Surveyor-General of Jersey for four years, a member of the Council, a judge of the Court of Common Pleas, and represented the County of Bergen in the House of Assembly. He was a churchman by profession, but gave land for a dissenting church at Hopewell, and for a Dutch Church at what is now Harlingen. He is said to have borne a bad character.—*Col. Hist. N. Y., vol. v., pp.* 204, 328, 535.

† Probably this tract had not been laid off to Arent Sonmans in his life-time. Peter may have inherited his father's interest, merely.

‡ Beginning at the south corner of a tract of land, of 3,000 acres, formerly laid out to Peter Sonmans, on the South Branch, fronting southeast by east, 3° more easterly, and running along the division line of

line, for six and a quarter miles, to a point directly
west of Blawenburg, and thence east and south-east, border-
ing on Dr. Greenland's land to the Millstone River, near
Rocky Hill, and thence down the river a mile and a half, to
the previous river grants (Benthall, etc.), and so along the
southerly and westerly sides of these, and the lands of Royce,
until it struck the Raritan, following which river and the
South Branch, and winding around a couple of plantations
previously ceded to Hooper* and Bennett, his bounds returned to Clover Hill, the place of beginning. Thus, our
township began to be ceded about 1683, and all its lands
had been actually taken up by individuals or companies by
1693, and the same was true of Montgomery township on
the south, and of Bridgewater on the north, at least to the

East and West Jersey six and a quarter miles, to the corner of William
Penn's land, thence east one and a half miles and five chains, east-south-
east two and a half miles and five chains, to north corner of Henry
Greenland's land, thence east by south along his line to Millstone
River, down said river one and a half miles, to upper corner of Walter
Benthall's land, thence opposite to the foot of Rocky Hills, thence west-
north-west two and three-quarter miles and two chains, north-north-east
three and three-quarter miles and three chains, east-south-east one mile
and eighteen chains, west by north one and three-eight miles, to south-
east corner of Thomas Cooper's land, west by north one mile and ten
chains, north by east two and a half miles and nine chains, to Raritan
River, up said River one-half mile and five chains, to corner of Dan.
Hooper's land, around which, south-west by south and north-west by
west, to the South Branch, up said Branch to the lower corner of Robt.
Bennett's land, thence south-east by east two miles, less six chains,
south-west by west one mile and six chains, thence west-south-west
to place of beginning, containing 23,000 acres.—*Deed in possession of
Peter A. Voorhees, Esq., of Six Mile Run.*

† Dan Hooper received 640 acres on Feb. 17th, 1692, beginning at
the junction of North and South Branches, running down the river about
half a mile, and up the South Branch about two miles.

Blue Hills, if not farther. The Millstone Valley began to be permanently settled about 1690, 176 years ago.*

Respecting the present Franklin township on the east (not including the Raritan lots before referred to,) there seem to be conflicting grants.† While Wm. Dockwra owned an immense tract, extending more than two miles along the Millstone, yet in or before the year 1700, John Harrison, of Flushing, Long Island, purchased of the Indians ‡ directly, a tract west of the Raritan lots, and apparently running back to the Millstone River, reaching nearly to Griggstown, on the river, and a little beyond Six Mile Run on the south-east. It embraced about 27 square miles. By or before the year 1700, therefore, all the neighboring territory was in the hands of Europeans. Royce and Sonmans, in the west, and Harrison and Dockwra, in the east, were among the first great landholders of the territory of our present congregation.

But the Government of New York was at this time administered by Governors appointed by the Crown, and was quite oppressive.§ The same was also true of New

---

* In the charter of the Church of Hillsborough, it is stated that the people of this place represent "That their ancestors and predecessors have been inhabitants of the township of Hillsborough and places adjacent, from the first Christian settlement of the colony."

† For further particulars, see *Early Records at New Brunswick, p.* 272.

‡ The Indian titles and those of the proprietors often conflicted. Royce is represented as a troublesome man, because he incited the people to hold their lands by the Indian titles alone.—*Whitehead's East Jersey, p.* 224.

Yet it is also known that Dockwra sold portions of Franklin township afterward.—*Papers of Jacob Wyckoff, of Middlebush.*

Some of his grants had been located here.

§ *Riker's Newtown, pp.* 101, 137, and the historical authorities generally.

England. East Jersey was governed in a totally different manner. It was comparatively a free State. The twenty-four proprietors failed not to disseminate information, not only concerning the climate and soil of Jersey, but also concerning the freedom of its government, which had been increased under their rule. The Dutch * around New York had always been dissatisfied with the encroachments of the English, since the conquest, not only politically, but also in their church affairs, the Church of England having been established by law. Many of them took advantage, therefore, of this opportunity to change their residence. Dutch companies and individuals soon began to buy tracts of various sizes of the original purchasers. Scotch and English emigrants also, who were exposed to not a little persecution from the national church at home, by the ship-load, arrived at Amboy, and penetrated up the Raritan.†

In 1742, (Feb. 28,) Clement Plumstead gave 2,900 acres of his land, including part of the territory of the present village of Millstone, to William Plumstead. Its northern bound was Peace Brook, and it extended up the river to Mr. Barker's land. In 1752, (May 1st,) Wm. Plumstead sold 246 acres of this plot, on the south of the Amwell road, to Christian Van Doren, for £740, and he three years later sold the same to his son, John Van Doren, for £100. Mr.

---

* The first Dutch on the Raritan came about 1683, and settled probably near its mouth.—See *Whitehead's East Jersey*, pp. 289, 294.

† The town of Piscataway received a charter in 1666 (*Whitehead's Amboy*, p. 401); and as early as 1680 there were some English plantations on the Raritan, below New Brunswick. Thomas Lawrence, a banker in New York, had 3,000 acres. Also at Raritan Landing, settlements had begun in this year (*Whitehead's East Jersey*, p. 92, 272). The last day of August, 1683, was set apart to meet the Indians and buy the lands at the head of the Raritan.—*Smith*.

Plumstead* had previously sold the strip between the Amwell road and Peace Brook, to Benjamin Thompson, while
Lawrence Van Cleef had bought (also previously), to the
south and west, of what now became the Van Doren tract.
Henry Vanderveer had purchased to the west of Thompson.

Early in the century, Mr. Dockwra had sold on the banks
of the Raritan and Millstone, 2,000 acres to John Covers
and John Brocars; † 1,800 acres to Van Wickland Bohoart,
400 to Thomas Purcell, 460 to Richard Davis, and 800 to
Evert Van Wickland.‡ He also sold a tract of 400 acres
up the Raritan, to Grotes Beckman and Evert Van Wickle,
of New York.§

In 1701 John Harrison sold a portion of his tract to a
Dutch company, consisting of Peter Cortelyou, Stoffel Probasco, Theodore Polhemus, Hendrick Lott, Hendrick Hen-
dricks, Jacques Cortelyou, and Dennis Tunis, all of Long

---

* Plumstead's land began at the mouth of Peace Brook, running along
said brook, west-north-west, 124 chains, south-south-west, 126, east-
south-east 206 chains, to Millstone River, opposite to Reverdie Brook,
and down the Millstone to the mouth of Peace Brook, leaving Barker
on the south, Reneer Veghte on the west, and Powelson and John Post
on the north.

† He was probably the ancestor of the Scotch Brokaws in this coun-
try. The French Huguenot Brokaw family originally wrote their name
Brogaw (see *Riker*), and in France, Broucard. Bourgon Broncard
came to America in 1675. He was born in 1645, and married Catherine
Le Febre. He left five sons and three daughters; Isaac (born 1676,) re-
mained on Long Island, while John (born 1678), Jacob (born 1680),
Peter (born 1682), and Abraham (born 1684), removed to Somerset
County, early in the last century.

‡ These sales of Dockwra were furnished by Mr. Wm. A. Whitehead,
from MSS. in his possession.

§ Trenton deeds in Secretary's office (I think). This last tract was
bounded south-east by Cover's and Brogaw's land; east and west by

Island.* They divided their plot into twelve equal lots,
and in 1703, Cor. Wyckoff,† of Long Island, joined the
party, purchasing lot No. 5 (1,200 acres), being in part the
farm now owned by Mr. Jacob Wyckoff, of Middlebush. It
then extended back to the Millstone. Still later, in 1723,
Christian Van Doren (before mentioned,) purchased‡ nearly
a square mile to the north of the present Middlebush church,
running back to the Raritan and Millstone lots, already laid
out. He came from Monmouth, whither the stream of
Dutch emigration from Long Island had first set.

The sales of John Royce are involved in considerable
perplexity, on account of conflicting grants, and human dishonesty. § Royce's patent originally took in, as we have
seen, a square of land between the Millstone and the Rari-

Dockwra's; south by land formerly owned by Stacklius; and north by
Rich. Davis' and Evert Van Wickle's land.

* *Papers of Jacob Wyckoff.* The next tract south, John Harrison
sold to Thos. Cardale, William Creed, Sam. Dean, Jona Wood and Sam.
Smith, in 1702, and Cardale sold his share to John Berrien in 1703.—
Early Rec. at New Brunswick, p. 272.

† He sold to his son John 300 acres for £200, who built a log house,
where Sam Garretson now lives. John's son, Cornelius, was the first
child born in Middlebush, and succeeded his father on this tract, dying
in 1795.—*Ralph Voorhees.*

The ancestor of the Wyckoff family came to this country in 1636
(Pieter Claesz Wyckoff), and settled at Flatlands. He married Grietje
Van Ness, and his sons were Claes, Hendrick, Cornelius, John, Gerrit,
Martin and Peter. (*Riker's Newtown, p.* 324.) This Cornelius is proba-
bly the one who bought land at Middlebush, in 1703.

‡ He appears to have purchased of Dockwra, from certain documents
in possession of Jacob Wyckoff, of Middlebush. It is also said that
the Van Dorens came to Monmouth direct from Holland.

§ Concerning Royce's dishonesty, see *Whitehead's East Jersey, p.* 224.
But Mr. Hamilton's references to the situation of the neighbors, upon
whom Royce encroached, do not seem to be in harmony with well-
known facts of their location.

tan, and extended from the covered bridge south and south-west for two miles, and thence east to the Millstone. But Mr. Royce fraudulently obtained another patent, still retaining his old, which extended his possessions three miles further up the Raritan, and to Peace Brook, in this village, (the brook flowing under the arch bridge,) encroaching greatly on Mr. Plumstead, on the south, and on Mr. Cooper on the west. While he originally received less than five square miles in 1685, in 1693 he leased about eight square miles of land for 1,000 years to Charles Winder,* for £206, with the privilege of redeeming it in three years. This he never did, but still continued to dispose of the lands, and the executors of both parties, after their deaths, claimed the same territory. In 1702, John Coevers (or Coevert,) bought 2,500 acres of Royce and Dockwra, on the Millstone and Royce's Brook; while in 1703, Andrew Coeymans, of Albany, bought 500 acres of Royce, it being stipulated in the deed that *that* tract especially should henceforth be called Roycefield.† This is the present district of that name.

Royce died in 1708, and his executors sold 1470 acres of his land to the east of Roycefield, and between the Raritan and

---

* *Early Rec. at New Brunswick*, p. 197. Though called a lease, it seems to have been of the nature of a mortgage.

† Royce was now living at Piscataway. This deed is dated June 2d, and the tract was sold for £80. Beginning at a small maple tree, at the mouth of a small stream of water, in a gully, by Ed. Drinkwater's land, then south ninety-one chains, west forty-eight chains, north 123 chains, north 3° west, twenty-three chains to the Raritan; then by said river west, six chains twenty-five links, south 3° east twenty-three chains, east six chains twenty-five links, to a walnut-tree, thence east by meadow land, formerly sold by Royce to Graham, and so to the place of beginning.— *Parchment Deed, Amboy.*

(These bearings are not altogether consistent, though copied correctly from the deed.)

Millstone Rivers and Royce's Brook, (to be henceforth known by the name of Royston,*) to Philip Hedman, for less than five dollars an acre; and four years later (1712) Hedman sold the same tract to Michael Van Vechty † and his associates, viz., Volkerse, Post, Allen, Wortman, Tunison, Andriese, and Van Nest. ‡ But this land, as well as the adjoining tract to the south, was now also claimed by the executors of Winder; and this Dutch company, having come in some way into possession of £500 of Royce's estate, from whom the land had been honestly purchased, with this money leased the two tracts § of Winder's executors for the yet unexpired term of Winder's lease—viz., 979

---

* Royce's executors were John Borron, John Harrison and Mary Crawley; besides the streams, on their sides, Royston is described as having the lands of John Van Dine and Ananias Allen, on the west. (Coeymans had probably sold a part of Roycefield to these. Hedman paid in all £1,850. Royce's will was written in 1706.—*Early Records at New Brunswick, p.* 174.

† *Early Rec. N. B., p.* 179. This Michael Van Vechty is not the one still remembered by some of the old people, but an ancestor of his. He also owned land on the north of the Raritan.

‡ A law was passed in 1694 to raise a tax of £150 in the province, and Peter Van Nest was appointed for Somerset. But the sparseness of population at this time is shown in that Somerset's proportion was only £4 16s 6d. While the other counties had their several towns, Somerset could not specify a single one. (Laws of State.) Rev. Rynier Van Nest (son of Peter,) was born in 1738, near the Raritan, and received the early part of his education under Rev. John Frelinghuysen. He was licensed in 1760.—*Riker's Newtown, p.* 242.

§ The tract leased by Royce to Winder in 1693, and now claimed by Winder's executors, and bought a second time by Van Vechty, is thus described: Beginning at the west end of an island in Raritan River, formerly owned by John Robinson, deceased, then south by west along Thomas Cooper's land, three miles, thence in a direct line to the head of a stream, now agreed to be called *Peace Brook*, being the north bound

years—binding themselves mutually to make up the £500, if Royce's heirs should ever recover it. Thus were the titles of Van Vechty & Co. made perfect. In 1703, therefore, the Dutch came into Roycefield, and in 1712 into Royston, a name now forgotten by the inhabitants of Harmony Plains.

On June 1st, 1702, John Covers bought of John Royce 512 acres of meadow land on Millstone River, then in the county of Middlesex. On March 6th, 1711, Covers sold this tract to William Post for £300.* The central portion of Peter Sonman's great tract of 23,000 acres in the west of this and the next township south, was sold to seventeen Dutch settlers in 1710.† The north-eastern corner of this

of Clement Plumstead's land, thence down said Brook to Millstone River, and down the Millstone four miles to the Raritan, and up the Raritan six and a half-miles to the place of beginning (excluding Graham's meadows, 250 acres). Winder died in 1710, and George Willocks was his executor. He gave a quit claim to Van Vechty & Co. for £555. *Early Rec. New Brunswick, pp. 192, 197.*

* *Early Records at New Brunswick, p. 160.* On June 10th, 1702, Thomas Cooper, of London, by his attorneys, Richard Hartshorne and Richard Salter, sold 2,000 acres on the south side of the Raritan, to Peter De Munt, for £380; beginning at a gully on said river, opposite the upper end of a great island (being also Royce's pretended bounds), thence south by west three miles (less ten chains), thence west by north one mile ten chains, thence north by east two and three quarter miles (less two chains), to Raritan River, and along said river to place of beginning.—*Early Record at New Brunswick, p. 171.*

† On June 10th. This is known as the 9,000 acre, or the Harlingen tract. It embraces a large section of Montgomery and Hillsborough townships, and contained 8,939 acres. The names of the parties were Octavio Conraats, Ab. Wendell, merchant, Adrian Hooghlandt, Isaac Governeur, all of city of New York; Anna Volkers, widow, of King's County, Long Island; Henry Hegeman, Francis Van Lewen, Wm. Beekman, all of Queen's County, Long Island; Joseph Hegeman,

tract reached to the present farm of Adrian Merrill, from
thence running west near to what is now Wood's tavern,
and thence **south-west** in a straight line to Rock Mills, about
seven miles ; while its eastern bound went in a straight line
from **said Adrian Merrill's** farm, striking and following **the**
present **road, which** is on **that** line, **to** the present farm of
Theodore Wyckoff, and **thence across** to the old Harlingen
Cemetery, and thence south-west and west to Rock Mills.
Among these seventeen purchasers, we find the names of
Veghte, **Cortelyou, Van Duyn,** Van Dike, Beekman, and
Hooglandt.　Thus came the Dutch into the western half of
our present township.*

This **great immigration and** settlement of this portion of
**New Jersey, began under the proprietors ; but while it was
progressing, they were induced by** certain embarrassments
which they experienced, to surrender their charter to the
crown.　This took place in 1702, and from that time till the
Revolution, New Jersey was under royal governors, being

Hendrick Veghte, **Cor. Van Duyn, Wouten Van** Pelt, Ort Van **Pelt,**
all of King's County, L. I. ; **Dirck Volkers, of New** Jersey ; Peter Cor-
telyou, Jacob Van Dyke, Claas Volkertse, all of King's County, L. I.
Bounded as follows :—Beginning at the south corner of land of William
Plumstead, being one and a half miles and four chains from Millstone
River (**by** what is now the new Amwell road) thence south-south-
west two and three-quarter miles and eight chains, west-north-west one
mile eighteen chains, south-south-west two and three-quarter miles and
seven **chains, west three** and a half miles and three chains, to the par-
tition line between East and West Jersey, thence north 14° west thirty
chains, north 53° east seven miles and twenty chains, east one mile and
seventeen chains, to place of beginning, having lands of Plumstead,
Barker, Hart and Benthall on the east, and the division line and other
lands of Peter Sonman on the west.

　* The Staats family settled on the farm now owned by Peter P.
Staats about 1730–40.—*Peter P. Staats.*

at times united to New York. Many Dutch families for
many years afterward, however, continued to remove to
this part of New Jersey, and to purchase lands of their former relatives, as well as from the English settlers, until in
time, it became almost altogether in possession of the
Dutch.* But it is plainly impracticable to trace this any
further in detail.

We now turn, after this perhaps too long introduction, to
the ecclesiastical history proper.

Churches and religious privileges did not by any
means. keep pace with the population.† Yet there was
a constant call among the people of all this State, for
religious teachers. All denominations were equally tole-
rated. The first minister in the State was Rev. Ab.
Pierson, of Newark, in 1666, a Presbyterian, and a church
was organized there the next year.

The country about Amboy and Elizabeth were very early
supplied to some extent, as before the year 1700, Fletcher
and Riddle, and Airsdale and Allen, and Drake and Harrison, and Shepherd,‡ had labored in that field, besides some
missionary Episcopalian efforts.§

The first Dutch minister in this State, was the Rev. Guilliam Bertholf, who preached for thirty years at Hackensack
and Aquacononck, beginning in 1694;‖ and in 1709, the

* In the charter of the five Collegiate Dutch churches in 1753, it is
represented that the Dutch are now very numerous in these localities,
and constantly increasing.

† See *Whitehead's East Jersey*, pp. 294, 302, 330, and his *History of
Perth Amboy*, p. 383.

‡ *Whitehead's Amboy*, pp. 28, 212, 371, 384, 404.

§ *Whitehead's Amboy*, pp. 209–212. *Whitehead's East Jersey*, p. 169.

‖ The church of Hackensack was founded in 1686, but the Dutch
church of Bergen is the oldest in the State, having been founded in
1660. The first Dutch minister in America was Jonas Michaelius, in

Dutch churches in Monmouth county, which had been earlier
settled, obtained the services of Rev. Joseph Morgan, who
labored there for twenty-two years. These two in New
Jersey, and never more at one time than two in New York
city, and two on Long Island (and at one period from
1702–1705, these four were reduced to one), constituted all
the Dutch ministers around New York city or in New
Jersey, being never more than six at one time; and indeed,
before the arrival of Frelinghuysen, in 1720, in these parts,
there had never been more than seven Dutch ministers at
the same time in America. How little divine service could
these then distant settlements enjoy!*

The church of Millstone is, indeed, one of the younger
Dutch churches in this section of the State, and it would be
a comparatively easy task simply to take up her history
from the organization; but such a plan would leave much
of the ecclesiastical history of the families now on our territory, in an obscurity, always unpleasant to the thoughtful
student, who is not satisfied with a work partially performed. A brief reference to the neighboring churches,
which for more than half a century the inhabitants of the
Millstone Valley attended, and with some of which they

1628. The settlers procured ministers from Classis of Amsterdam, in
Holland, through the West India Co.

Taylor's Annals of Classis of Bergen, p. 174.
Col. His. N. Y., vol. ii., pp. 759–770.

* Gualterus Dubois labored in New York from 1699 to 1751; Bernardus Freeman, on Long Island, from 1705 to 1741; Vicentius Antonides, also on Long Island, being colleague with the former, from 1705
to 1744; and Henricus Boel, in New York, as colleague with Dubois
from 1713 to 1754. These were the only Dutch ministers, in the
vicinity of New York, in the first quarter of the last century, and from
these, and the two in Jersey, all the help must have come.

several times conjointly called a pastor, will surely not be deemed inappropriate.*

About 1699, Rev. Guilliam Bertholf, the only Dutch minister then in New Jersey, organized the church of Raritan. The place of worship stood at first and until the Revolution, just over the Raritan, near the residence of the late Mr. Dunn. But in 1703, we find also a church organization, and probably a building, at Three Mile Run, where the old grave-yard yet remains ; for in that year, we find a list of persons subscribing to the amount of £10 16s. and 6d. to pay the expenses of a minister from Holland. These were families† who had settled on the Harrison tract, and on the Raritan lots, and some few from beyond the Millstone. But no pastor could be procured till 1720, when Rev. T. J. Frelinghuysen arrived. But in the meantime (1717‡), the little church of Three Mile Run, sent out two colonies, establishing from itself the churches of New Brunswick and Six Mile Run. And about the same time, or a little after, a Dutch church was organized at the

---

* The large correspondence of the Classis of Amsterdam, in Holland, with the Dutch churches in this country, will no doubt throw considerable light upon the history of all these early churches. It will soon be accessible to the public.

                              See Mints. of Gen. Syn. for 1866, p. 112.

† Their names were —— Hegeman, Tunis Quick, Hend. Emens, Thos. Cort, Jac. Probasco, Neclas Wyckoff, —— avi L. Draver, Mic. L. Moore, John Schedemeun, Nec. Van Dike, John Van Houten, Wil. Bennet, Folkert Van Nostrand, Jac. Bennet, Hend. Fanger, Ab. Bennet, Cor. Peterson, Philip Folkerson, Geo. Anderson, Stobel Probasco, Isaac Le Priere, Simon Van Wicklen, Cobes Banat, Garret Cotman, Lucas Coevert, Brogun Coevert, Wil. Van Duin, Dennis Van Duin, John Folkerson, Jost. Banat.

‡ Possibly Six Mile Run was organized as early as 1710. I am told there was a letter published in the " Christian Intelligencer " some years ago, stating such a fact, derived from some records in Bucks County, Pa.; but I have not seen it.

Branches of the Raritan, called the church of North Branch, and which, in 1738, was removed to Readington.

Thus by the **year 1720**, there were no less than five Dutch churches on the Raritan and its branches, plainly showing that in the twenty years preceding, there had been a large immigration of Dutch from New York and Long Island. A Mr. Alexander, in writing to ex-Governor Hunter, in 1730, says that the road from Brunswick to the Delaware is lined with white fences, and comfortable looking farm-houses; whereas, in 1715, when he traveled that road before, there were only four or five houses between the Raritan and the Delaware. The country was then, however, as we have already seen, and as the list for Three Mile Run proves, more thickly settled back in Franklin township, and along the Raritan. Do. Frelinghuysen lived a little west of Three Mile Run, proving probably that the main part of his people lived in that vicinity, and his grave is pointed out in that locality to this day, though without a stone to mark the spot.*

We cannot, of course, go into his history in detail,† as all that is known of him has been published in various forms heretofore. Suffice it to say, that the long lack of frequent religious services had produced a most lamentable declension in the piety of the people, which had perhaps been

---

* Do. Frelinghuysen lived in the place now owned by John Bronson. —*R. Voorhees, of Middlebush.*

† He was born at Lingen, in East Friesland, Hanover, about 1691. He was ordained in Friesland in 1717, by John Brunius, and settled at Embden. The churches of the Raritan obtained Mr. Frelinghuysen through the kind offices of Rev. Mr. Freeman, of Long Island, who also afterward vindicated him from the aspersions of his enemies.

See *Frelinghuysen's Sermons*, pp. 5, 7, 299, 357.
Messler's Memorial, Taylor's Annals, p. 176.
Gunn's Livingston, p. 359.

somewhat formal before, and Frelinghuysen, being thoroughly evangelical, and bold withal,* not sparing their sins of any kind, necessarily aroused great opposition, (1723.) But in the strength of God he persevered, and maintained his position to the end, and succeeded in impressing upon the new generation, his own deeply religious character; and now for his fidelity, he is universally honored by the descendants of those who once opposed him.

It was during his time, also, that the Dutch denomination became rent into two factions—the Coetus, representing the thoroughly evangelical party, the party of progress and reform, and to which Frelinghuysen contributed not a little ;† and the Conferentie, as the other party was called, representing formality, and adherence to custom, and horror at innovation,‡ even when change would be undeniable

---

* His enemies shut his churches against him, so that he had to preach in barns, in 1725. In the same year a slanderous book appeared against him, and afterward a lawsuit was begun, to try to eject him, but he was acquitted by the court ; they also complained of him to the Classis of Amsterdam, but they sustained him. New Brunswick is not named in the protest against him.

Frelinghuysen's Sermons, pp. 7, 8, 353.

Whitehead's East Jersey, pp. 168, 291, 305–7.

† Mr. Frelinghuysen was one of the originators of the Coetus, in 1738; the eminent and useful elder, Hendrick Fisher, of New Brunswick, accompanying him. The text in Mints. of Gen. Syn., vol. i., pp. 8, 13, does not decide whether the Frelinghuysen who is there said not to have won over his consistory yet to the Coetus, is Theodore of Raritan or John of Albany.

‡ Both the Frelinghuysens had helpers, (like the Apostles,) to partially supply their places when absent; but some found great fault with this innovation. The Conferentie, seeing their waning influence, became at last unwilling to have the majority rule.—*Mints. Gen. Syn.* vol. i., p. 96., and *Messler's Memorial.*

improvement. For fifty years did the strife continue,
which was often very bitter, all the churches in this
county having two consistories,[*] representing, respectively,
the progressive and the unprogressive parties. And it was
only through the changes brought about by the American
Revolution, that this strife was at length effectually
allayed.[†]

It was during the first Frelinghuysen's ministry, moreover, that the church at what is now called Harlingen was
formally organized, although for some cause, not now well
understood, he himself was not invited to do this work,
though it lay within his pastoral field.[‡] Rev. Henricus
Coens, who had commenced to labor during the preceding
year at Aquacononck, ordained the Consistory on May 18th,
1727. They called themselves the church "*over the Millstone*,"[§] indicating apparently thereby, that the inhabitants

---

[*] *Mints. Gen. Syn.*, vol. i., p. 103. *Gunn's Livingston*, pp. 141–143.
Harlingen Records, 1734.

Kain, the Swedish traveler, in 1728, speaks of one Presbyterian and
two German (Dutch?) churches in New Brunswick. Possibly the Consistory was divided, or Kain may have been mistaken.

[†] The Conferentie frequently refused to recognize the ministers of the
Coetus as legitimate, but God had received them, and they finally pre-
vailed. While negotiations were progressing for several years before,
to free the American churches from infantile dependence on Holland,
the independence of the country settled the matter forever.

[‡] *See Mints. Gen. Syn.*, vol. i., p. 4, respecting this church, under the
younger Frelinghuysen.

[§] Die Kerk op der Millstone. The name *Millstone*, applied to the
river, occurs in the first references to this section of country. There is
a tradition, (though not very reliable,) that a millstone was once lost in
the river, when crossing a bridge, and never recovered, and hence the
name. Scot, writing in 1685, says that the hills on the north were
filled with good millstones, (*Whitehead's East Jersey*, p. 265,) and this
may have suggested the name for this branch of the Raritan; but it is

of that region had previously attended church at Six Mile
Run. It was known by the name of the Church of Millstone,* and afterwards sometimes by the name of Sourland,
until after the death of the elder Rev. Van Harlingen,
when out of memory to him, and to distinguish it from our
own village, it became incorporated, under the name of
Harlingen, in 1801. It was soon after organization, very
largely increased in numbers, and prospered much. Fifty-
three members were received in the first twenty years. It
began with only seven. †

Two years after the organization of what is now the
church of Harlingen, (viz., 1729,) the old church of Three
Mile Run, although Frelinghuysen was living close by,
made an effort to call a minister for themselves ; and since
they were not acting in concert with the other churches,
but alone, it would seem, that it must have been disaffection on their part toward the faithful Frelinghuysen. In
the same document,‡ the church building at that place is

also sometimes early spelled as mile-stone, perhaps a mile-stone on
some route, standing on its banks, and in what place so likely, as where
the road from Brunswick to Trenton crosses the Millstone, near Princeton, that being just twenty miles from the Raritan? This is the most
probable derivation. The present village of Millstone is frequently
called Middleburgh in early deeds.

* "The Church of Millstone," in all records before 1766, and sometimes after, means the church now at Harlingen. Hence the error in
the Manual of R. P. D. C., which dates the organization of Millstone in
1727, the writer not then being acquainted with these localities.

† For a fuller account of the church of Harlingen, see Christopher C.
Hoagland's pamphlet.

‡ Papers in possession of Hon. Ralph Voorhees, of Middlebush.
Henry Vroom and Fred. Van Liew were appointed a committee to
carry out these matters, if successful, in procuring a minister. The following names are attached to the salary-list for this call: —— A.
Boorham, Simon Wyckoff, Dennis Van Duyn, —— Smock, Cor. Peter-

represented as old and dilapidated, and they agree, if they
secure a minister, to build a new place of worship shortly,
to be located on the lands of John Pittenger, at Three Mile
Run. But they did not procure a new minister, and probably the new building was never begun, and with the
disuse of the old, the church in that place expired. The
last reference to it is in 1751.* For a long time previous,
it had had two consistories.

Dos. Antonides, De Ronde, and Arondeus,† of Long
Island, were the troublesome men, who visited all the
churches in Frelinghuysen's field several times a year.
They were formal and unevangelical men themselves,
organizing consistories, which were opposed to the regular
consistories,‡ and baptizing the children of the disaffected.§
These actions began in 1734, and thirteen years later,
Arondeus permanently removed to these parts, and died
in 1754. But the locality of his home and grave are
unknown.

After the death∥ of Rev. T. J. Frelinghuysen. about

son, Geo. Anderson, Wm. Van Duyn, Jac. Boise, Hen. Smock, Chris.
Probasco, Wm. Kouwenhoven, Jac. Bennet, Pet. Bodine, Gid. Marlat,
Wm. Bennet, Paul Le Boyton, Francis Harrison, Ab. Bennett, Isaac
Le Queer, Jac. Bennet, —— ——, Nic. Daily, Ad. Hardenbrook, Luke
Covert, Jac. Probasco.

* See *Mints. Gen. Syn.*, vol. i., pp. lv., cxxxi.
† See *Mints. of Gen. Syn.*, vol. i., session of 1751.
‡ See vol. i. *Gen. Syn.*, pp. cxxxi., ciii., lv., lvi., for fuller particulars.
§ The Harlingen Records have a list of baptisms by Arondeus, from
1744 to 1749, including certain baptisms at Raritan.—*Frelinghuysen's
Sermons*, pp. 355–58.
See also the second paragraph of p. 340, and pp. 354, 358, of *Freling-
huysen's Sermons*. Mr. Frelinghuysen called him a *dead man*.
∥ He left five sons and two daughters ; viz., Theodore, who preached
at Albany, 1745–1760, when he went to Holland to raise funds for a

1747, the churches of New Brunswick and Six Mile Run conjointly called Rev. John Leydt, who was one of the students prepared and examined by the Coetus in this country. His call was approved, September 27, 1748.

The other three churches, viz., Raritan, Harlingen and Readington, united and called Rev. John Frelinghuysen,* the son of their preceding pastor, and who arrived in this country in August, 1750. He lived near Somerville.

During his time, the people of Harlingen built a new church near the present site, leaving the land originally given to them, where the cemetery remains. The youthful pastor dedicated the new building in 1752, preaching from the texts—1 Kings viii. 29, and Psalm xxvii. 4: "That thine eyes may be open toward this house, night and day, even toward the place of which Thou hast said, My name shall be there: that thou mayest hearken unto the prayer which thy servant shall make toward this place." And, "One thing have I desired of the Lord, that will I seek after, that I may dwell in the house of the Lord all the days of my life, to behold the beauty of the Lord, and to inquire in His temple."

During the ministry of Leydt and the younger Frelinghuysen, in 1753, the five Dutch churches over which they presided, obtained a common charter, including them all under one corporation.

But the youthful Frelinghuysen's labors were not long in

literary institution, and on his return was lost at sea; John, who succeeded his father in Somerset County; Jacob and Ferdinand, died at sea on their return from Holland in 1753; Henry, who settled at Warwarsing and Rochester in 1756, and died in 1757; Anna, married Rev. Wm. Jackson, of Bergen, and Margaret married Rev. Thos. Romeyn, of Long Island.

* See *Mints. Gen. Syn.*, vol. l., pp. liii., xcvii.

the church below.   After only four years of service, and at
the early age of twenty-eight, he died.   This took place in
September, 1754.*   An effort was then made by the church
of North Branch, to induce the united congregations to call
Rev. John C. Freyenmoet, who had been preaching for ten
years at Minisink and connected places, on the upper
waters of the Delaware.   And though there was a strong
party in his favor in each of the churches, they did not
succeed in their design,† having their eye already on
Mr. Jacob R. Hardenbergh, who had married young Frelinghuysen's widow.   In the meantime, in 1758, the churches
of Nechanic and Bedminster were organized, and these two,
in connection with the other three, in the same year called
Mr. Hardenbergh, (who was ordained in October,) and
who served the three northern churches, (with the exception of a visit to Holland of two years,) for twenty-three
years.   But Sourland and Nechanic, during his absence,
called Rev. John M. Van Harlingen,‡ in 1761,§ and he
served these two churches till his death, in 1795, the people
making great lamentation over him.

In 1759,‖ the year after Mr. Hardenbergh had been called

* He died suddenly on Long Island, while there to attend the
Coetus.—*Min. Gen. Syn.*, p. lxxxix.
He left one son, Frederick, who was the father of the late Hon.
Theodore Frelinghuysen.

† They had only three or four services in two years, after Frelinghuysen's death.—*Mints. Gen. Syn.*, vol. i., pp. ciii., xcix.

‡ He was a native of Millstone, but had gone to Holland to be
educated.

§ *Doc. Hist. N. Y.*, vol. i., p. 406.   He was no doubt a descendant of
Frans Van Harlingen, of Holland, with whom Dr. Livingston frequently
stayed when in that country.—*Gunn's Livingston*, p. 80.

‖ Rev. Wm. Jackson, of Bergen, a great field orator, and second only

to the five churches north and west of the Raritan and the Millstone, the English settlers of Millstone petitioned to have regular preaching in this locality.* While we have been tracing the history of the Dutch Presbyterians, we must remember that the English Presbyterians were increasing in even a more rapid ratio. The Presbytery of New Brunswick had been organized since 1738, and all around, Presbyterian churches had sprung up. Many ship-loads of persecuted dissenters, from England and Scotland, had arrived at Amboy, and moved directly up the Raritan, and were the founders of the early Presbyterian churches in our county,† and these are represented, by early writers, as persons who had been refined and purified by afflictions and persecutions.

to Whitefield, was called in this year as a colleague with Hardenbergh, but did not accept.—*Taylor's Annals*, p. 125.

* *Rec. Presbytery of New Brunswick.* The Presbytery met at Basken-ridge, Oct. 30th, 1759. It then consisted of Revs. John Guild, Israel Reed, Benj. Hart, Sam. Kennedy, Sam. Harker, Wm. Tennent, David Cowl, Chs. McKnight, Jas. McCrea, Thos. Lewis, John Prudden, and Conrad Wortz, besides elders.

† The first Presbytery organized in America was that of Philadelphia in 1705. The Wall-street Presbyterian church, (the first in city of New York,) was organized in 1716. (*Doc. Hist.*, iii., 79. *Riker's Newtown*, p. 138.) The Long Island Presbytery was organized in 1717, taking in New York and Westchester. That of East Jersey a little later, and that of New Brunswick in 1738. This Presbytery, at its organization, included the following churches in this vicinity:—Paepack, Crosswick's, Cranberry, Maidenhead, Hopewell, Bound Brook, Baskenridge, Leba-non, Readington, Neshaminy, and New Brunswick. (See *Whitehead's East Jersey*, pp. 204, 257, 268. *Whitehead's Amboy*, pp. 23, 35. *Smith's New Jersey*, p. 166.) This rapid immigration, and the feelings of the immigrants themselves, show a powerful religious prescience, that God intended America as the field for the development of liberty and religion. Compare Rev. xii., which certainly received its crowning fulfillment, in the flight of the many religious exiles to these shores.

The Dutch and English in this vicinity therefore united, and built a common place of worship, about 1760.

Eleven years before, the Presbyterian church of Bound Brook had called and settled a young man by the name of Israel Read, and now the Presbyterians of this place enter into an engagement with the church of Bound Brook,* to secure a service once a month. The Dutch also held service about as often in the same building, which stood on the present premises of Mr. Van Mater Van Cleef, of this village. Dos. Leydt, Van Harlingen, and especially Hardenbergh, preached for them in this place.

After a few years, however, some difficulty occurred between the parties, in reference to the church building, the points of which have not been distinctly ascertained, and the Dutch resolved to build a church edifice for themselves. Mr. Israel Read† served the English in this place for about nine years, after which he divided his labors between Bound Brook and New Brunswick, till 1786, when Rev. Walter Monteith succeeded him in the latter place. Mr. Read continued at Bound Brook till 1793, when he was killed by being thrown from his wagon at Raritan landing, November 28, 1793, being in his seventy-fifth year.‡ After he ceased to preach in Millstone, about

* The Presbyterian church of Bound Brook was organized about 1700, and that of Baskenridge in 1732. English and Scotch Presbyterians began to locate on the Raritan as early as 1683, the first ones coming from Amboy, Woodbridge and vicinity.—*Dr. Rogers' Hist. Sermon of Bound Brook.*

† Rev. Mr. Lamb, of Baskenridge, occasionally, and Rev. Mr. Crea, from about 1745-'50, supplied the Presbyterian church of Bound Brook before the settlement of Mr. Reed.

‡ His successors were—Rev. David Barclay, 1794-1805; Rev. Selah Strong Woodhull, 1805-1806, when he went to R. D. C., of Brooklyn; Rev. Jas. Paterson, 1809-1813; Rev. Wm. A. McDowell, 1813-1814;

1769, they had supplies occasionally,* from the neighboring Presbyterian churches, until the Revolution, and between the close of that event, and the beginning of this century, a Rev. Mr. Elmore,† from Elizabethtown, preached here a part of his time, as tradition says, though no documentary evidence concerning him at this time, has been met with.

After the Revolution, considerable correspondence ‡ took place between the Presbytery of New Brunswick, and the Classis of New Brunswick, respecting this Presbyterian church in Millstone; but the early books and papers of Classis, which contained this correspondence, are lost,—said to have been destroyed by fire. The Dutch complained that the Presbyterians encroached on their territory, and committees of conference were appointed. But the Presbyterian congregation gradually dwindled, until it became extinct. The building, no longer safe, was taken down about 1809.§

On July 26th, 1766, seventy heads ‖ of families of the

Rev. John Boggs, 1815–1828; Rev. Dr. Rodgers, 1830 to present time. —*Dr. Rodgers' MSS. Sermons.*

* In 1770 the licentiate, Wm. Schenck, supplied them two Sabbaths, and subsequently Rev. Sam Kennedy, of Baskenridge, Rev. Mr. Van Arsdale, and Rev. Mr. Smith, of Cranberry. In 1775 this Presbyterian church united with Kingston in calling a man, but without success; on April 23d, 1776, they petitioned for a minister to assist Mr. Elmore in the celebration of the Lord's supper, (hence Mr. Elmore must have been at this time unlicensed,) and Mr. Kennedy was appointed.

† He died between sixty and seventy years ago.

‡ *Mints. Gen. Syn.*, vol. i., pp. 104, 108.

§ It was a small building with a very steep roof. It is said that the land belonging to it, having been sold, the proceeds were divided among the heirs of the original donor, by the name of Ten Eyck.

‖ Peter Schenck, Cornelius Van Liew, Hend. Probasco, Ab. Van Beuren, Hend. Schenck, Jice Smock, John Vanderveer, Lawr. Van

Dutch settlers of the Millstone Valley, addressed a petition to the Dutch ministers and elders of Raritan, New Brunswick, Six Mile Run, and Millstone, (i. e. now Harlingen,) as follows:—"We, the undersigned, belonging to the aforesaid congregations, and living where the four congregations meet, finding it very inconvenient, and sometimes impossible to attend the Dutch church or Dutch services with our families, which, in view of God's command, and our baptizmal vows, we feel to be the duty of ourselves and children, and also for other reasons which we might present; therefore we have deliberated, whether a new congregation ought not to be established by taking some from each of these congregations; and having considered it advisable, we request respectfully your council and advice. If our desire be approved, (and our prayer is that it may prosper,) and we on the Lord's day, once a month, or as often as possible, may be served, by our three ministers; then, for the accomplishment of the same, we will provide a place of worship, and salary. This petition, we sign with respect,

Cleef, Ram. Ditmars, Bergen Coevert, Jr., Sam. Brewer, John Van Doren, John Smock, Peter Stryker, Dan. Covert, Jac. Wyckoff, Jac. Van Noorstrandt, Hend. Wilson, Jer. Douty, John Stryker, Cor. Lott, John Probasco, Christiaen Van Doren, Ab. Van Doren, Phil. Folkerson, John Blauw, Pet. Blauw, Ab. Metzelaer, Peter Perrine, Burgon Hoff, Jer. Silwill, Jac. Stryker, Wm. Geo. Prall, Mary Arrismith, Jac. Metzelaer, Aron Van Dorn, Wm. Spader, Pet. Cavaleer, Peter Wilson, John Christopher, John Brokau, John Hoogeland, John Covert, Mindert Wilson, Isaac Brokau, Joseph Arrismith, Joseph Vanderveer, Rem. Gerritson, Juryee Van Cleef, Dirrick Croesen, Peter Wyckoff, John Powelson, Stephen Turhune, Douwe Ditmars, Hend. Vanderveer, Luke Rynierson, Reynier Van Hengelen, Sam. Gerretson, Jac. Gerritson, Stoffel Van Arsdalen, Gerret Turhune, Jos. Cornel, Barent Stryker, Gretje Cornel, John Ditmars, Roelof Turhune, Marritje Van Nuys, Wm. Corteljou.

submission and love, praying God Almighty to overrule all things for the best.

" And furthermore, the salary, as is usual, shall be paid by each one of us. The Rev. ministers, above mentioned, are invited, with elders from each of the congregations, to come together at the house of Peter Schenck, on Monday, the eleventh of August, prox."

Accordingly on the eleventh of August, 1766, Rev. John Leydt, pastor of the churches of New Brunswick and Six Mile Run, with an elder respectively from each, viz., Hendrick Fisher, and Ab. Voorheese; Rev. Jacob R. Hardenbergh, of Raritan, with the elder Reynier Van Neste; and the Rev. J. M. Van Harlingen, of Nechanic and Sourland, with elders Simon Van Arsdalen, and Johannes De Mott, met together at the house of Peter Schenck, (which stood on the present premises of Deacon Broach,) and after prayer, each of the points of the petition were thoroughly discussed, and the petition and plan were approved; except that the new congregation should not have the services of the three ministers without the consent of their respective congregations, as it would infringe on their calls. They at once proceeded to erect a Consistory, and to establish the congregation under the name of NEW MILLSTONE. They accordingly elected Joseph Cornell and Peter Schenck for elders, and Johannes Hogelandt, and Ab. Van Beuren, M.D., for deacons. Dominie Leydt, of New Brunswick, was appointed to ordain the new Consistory on a certain day, the date of which is not given, but being prevented by an accident, this duty was performed by Dominie Hardenbergh, of Raritan.

A little difficulty was at once experienced in reference to the bounds of the new congregation, as the Consistories of each of the other churches complained that it was taking too many families from them.* Accordingly each Consistory determined what families could be spared, and no others should attempt to go, and those who were permitted to go, should also have the privilege of remaining in their old connections if they chose. Our Consistory protested that these arrangements very much contracted them, but still promised to do nothing to disturb the peace.

The three neighboring ministers, by an arrangement entered into with their congregations, each preached at New Millstone four times a year, giving them conjointly a service once a month. Thus matters stood for eight years.

The first thing the new consistory attempted to do, was to erect a house of worship, in accordance with their promise, and also because it was not agreeable longer to use the Presbyterian edifice, which it would seem from the withdrawal of the Dutch, had been built chiefly by the English. A subscription was begun, in December of the same year, which received seventy-eight names,† and an aggregate amount of £446 or $1,115 00, the subscribers agreeing to pay the sums promised, in four installments of six months each, beginning May 1st, 1767. The subscription paper states that the Church should be built on a piece of land near the Somerset Co. Court House, (this being the County-seat,) which land should be bought by the builders of John Smock. It was further stipulated, that the congregation should belong to the Coetus, i. e., the progressive party in the church, showing that the efforts of the First Frelinghuysen, on the people of this locality, had not been

* This subject was agitated for many years. In 1790 the road running west from the brick-walled cemetery, was made the division line between Raritan and Millstone, Weston also being included in Raritan. *Consist. Book* 2. *p.* 13.

† See Appendix. Note 1.

in vain. Subscriptions * were also solicited for help in New-York and on Long Island, and £104 10s. 11d. or $260 were thus received for the original building of the Church.

John Van Doren gave land to the church immediately north of the present parsonage lot, on what is now the garden of Dr. Fred. Blackwell. But John Smock, who owned the plot where the church now stands, being willing to exchange with the Consistory, they gladly accepted of the proposal, on account of the superiority of the site, and hence the deed for the ground stands in the name of John Smock, dated Jan. 7th, 1767, to certain trustees,† in behalf of the congregation. The land comprised eight and a half tenths of an acre, and was valued at £10. This plot was subsequently increased, by three different purchases of land, viz., the square west of the Lecture Room of Dan. Disborough, in 1814,‡ the western end of the grave-yard of John Broach, in 1834,§ and a small plot in the northwest corner of the yard, of Dan. Disborough, in 1835, ‖ costing in all $191.

---

* The Committee to build the Church consisted of Rem Ditmars, Hendrick Willson, Jan Probasco, Jan Vanderveer, Cor. Van Lewen, Hend. Probasco, and John Van Doren.

† These were Rem Ditmars, Hend. Willson, John Probasco, John Vanderveer, Cor. Van Lewe, John Van Doren, and Hend. Probasco. Bounded as follows :—Beginning at a point in Benj. Thompson's line, thence north $87\frac{1}{4}°$ east, 3 chains and 14 links, to the middle of the road, south $2\frac{1}{2}°$ west, 3 chains, to John Van Doren's line, along which south $87\frac{1}{2}°$ west, 2 chains, 75 links, north $9\frac{3}{4}°$ west, 3 chains, to place of beginning.

‡ This was a rectangle of 38×72 feet, and cost $40.

§ Beginning in the Amwell road in Van Doren's line, north $4\frac{1}{2}°$ west, 3 chains, 4 links, to Disborough's line, along which north $87\frac{1}{4}°$ east, 46 links, thence south 10° east, 3 chains, 6 links, to Amwell road, and up said road north 87° west, 75 links, to place of beginning, containing 2-10 of an acre.

‖ Beginning at north-east corner of John Broach's lot, being also a corner of Disborough's lot, north $4\frac{1}{4}°$ west, 57 links, north $87\frac{1}{2}°$ east,

These several plots together constitute the present church-yard, including a little more than an acre.

This first house of worship was probably completed within a year and a quarter from the organization of the church. Its breadth, like many of the old churches, was greater than its depth. It contained in all sixty-six pews, two being reserved by the pulpit for the Consistory, one by the west wall, (the wall pews faced the congregation.) for the justice, and two tiers or eight pews in the back of the church, were free. A stairway ran up in the south-west corner to the belfry. The church contained three aisles, and two large pillars arose, in the midst of either block of pews, to support the roof. This building, though considerably damaged by fire in the Revolution, and having undergone a couple of thorough repairings, stood for sixty years.

The baptismal register of the church begins April 3d, 1767, when Eva, daughter of Dr. Van Beuren, one of the deacons, was baptized, and baptisms occur afterwards every few months, showing regular services. But only fifteen formed the original membership of the church, including officers, and ten were added by profession and two by certificate, during the period that they remained without a pastor.*

53 links, to a corner of Phebe Lott's lot, south 4° east, 57 links, south 87½° west, 53 links, to place of beginning, containing 3-100 of an acre. $1.

The plot now occupied by the lecture-room, was given by Dan. Disborough for a school lot, in 1814. It is 130×38 feet. In 1860, by an act of the Legislature, the school district obtained power to sell this lot, that they might locate the school on the hill, north of the town ; it was bought by certain trustees in behalf of the members of the congregation of Hillsborough, living in school district No. 3, to be used by them for educational and moral purposes.

* Our Consistory paid to each of the neighboring Consistories about $40 a year, for the services of their ministers.

It was also during this time, that the great convention of Dutch ministers and elders was held in New York, for the purpose of consummating the independence of the Dutch churches in America, of the parent church in Holland. Peter Schenck, of this church, signed the articles,* which bound the conflicting parties, to union and peace, in behalf of the church of New Millstone, the Coetus having at last triumphed in their reformatory efforts.

It is probable that at this convention, (October, 1772,) Mr. Schenck, the elder from this place, became acquainted with Rev. Christian F. Foering, then preaching in the German church in the city of New York, and which ultimately resulted in Mr. Foering's settling at Millstone. He was first called in November, 1773, as a colleague of Do. Hardenbergh, of Raritan, the two churches uniting in the call. They promised him £130, a house, and sixty acres of land, and urged him strongly to accept. But his congregation in New York being very feeble, and his Consistory fearing that their church would die if he left, he resolved to his own temporal discomfort to remain in New York.

The congregation of New Millstone, notwithstanding their ill success in procuring at present the services of Mr. Foering, did not despair.

In the summer of 1774, (July 23d,) they bought a parsonage farm in two unequal plots, containing about fifty-three acres, and for which they gave bonds to nine individuals, (of whom they borrowed money to pay for it,) amounting to £348. Four and a half acres additional were added the next spring. It is the place now occupied by John Henry

* At this convention, the Circle (or Classis,) of New Brunswick was organized, 1771. The first volume of their minutes, reaching from 1771-1811, is lost, and thus probably much material, which might have been used profitably in this history.

Wilson, Esq., of this township.* The two larger plots were bought of Peter Wilson,† the smaller one of John Bannett.

* The trustees for this farm were Peter Schenck, Esq., Jos. Cornell, Ernestus Van Harlingen, Johannes Hoagland, Dr. Ab. Van Beuren, John Probasco, Dr. Lawrence Vanderveer, Cor. Lott, Hend. Wilson, Cor. Van Lewe, Hend. Probasco, John Van Doren, Ram Ditmars, John Smock, John Stryker, Garret Terhune, Jr., John Bennett, and Wm. Van Doren. Bounded as follows:—Beginning on the Millstone at the south-east corner of lands of Hend. Willson, west along his line 11 chains, on the edge of the upland, north 22° east, 5 chains, 75 links, north 89° west, 33 chains, 35 links, to the middle of the road that leads from the Somerset Court House to the Raritan; along said road south 17¼° west, 12 chains, to north-west corner of Cor. Lott's land; along his line north 87¾° east, 28 chains, 40 links, to a corner of John Bennett's land; along his line north 1° west, 1 chain, 92 links, thence north 87¾° east, 2 chains, 60 links, south 54° east, 12 chains, 40 links, to the Millstone River, along which 10 chains 82 links to place of beginning, containing 42 2-10 acres. *Also,* another lot, beginning at a stake, thence north 89° east, along Hend. Willson's line, 24 chains, 58 links, south 10° east, along Isaac Van Huys' line, 4 chains, south 87½° west, 24 chains, 58 links, along line of Ernest. Van Harlingen, north 4° west, along Cor. Lott's line, 3 chains, 40 links, to place of beginning, containing 9 1-10 acres. On May 1st, 1775, John Bennett sold an additional lot to the parsonage for £30, on the south-east corner, as follows:— Beginning at north-east corner of Cor. Lott's land at Millstone River, north 53½° west, 9 chains, 50 links, north 30′ west, 2 chains, 44 links, south 77½° west, 2 chains, 56 links, to a corner of the Parsonage farm, along Parsonage line north 30′ west, 1 chain 92 links, north 77½° east, 2 chains, 60 links, south 53½° east, 12 chains 40 links, to a corner of Parsonage, thence down the Millstone to the place of beginning, containing 4½ acres, and 20 perches.

† Hendrick Wilson had come from Long Island in the second quarter of the last century. He was born about 1680, and died in 1750. He bought a large tract of land, (probably of Michael Van Vechty,) and by will directed it to be divided between his four sons, and daughter, giving to Myndert £20 additional, as his birthright. Myndert, (born about 1716, died about 1800,) received the western part, and lived

The house was at once repaired, Henry Wilson, Peter Stryker, Sr., John Stryker, Henry Probasco, and Lawrence Van Cleef, being the building committee, and when ready for use, the Consistory found themselves indebted £393. The final payment was made in 1779.* In the fall of 1774, therefore, they renew their invitation to Mr. Foering, and this time with better success. He accepted of this call in the early part of October, 1774, and moved the following month. He states in a letter, that the low Dutch language was rapidly passing away in Millstone, and that he was called to preach altogether in English.

Christian Frederick Foering was born in Hanover about 1736. His father was a soldier in that kingdom, (at this time united to the English crown,) and died in the military service. His mother was a woman of great energy, and looked with dread to the time when her son should grow up to manhood, only to be impressed into the army, and perhaps to lose his life, in some of the petty personal disputes of princes and kings. She therefore determined to leave the country, with her only son, and seek for him liberty, and a proper chance in the race of life, in the wilds of America. But it was difficult to escape with one, who would in due time become subject to military duty, yet she devised a plan. She tied her boy, then seven years old, to

where now lives Mr. French; John lived on what is now the farm of Albert Voorhees; Hendrick lived on the present place of Jas. Elmendorf, (died about 1802,) and who gave about $1000 to the church, which, with other legacies, has been invested in successive parsonages; and Peter, (not yet of age in 1750,) who lived on the present place of John H. Wilson, and who sold a part of his land in 1774 for a parsonage. Myndert left four sons—Hendrick, William, Myndert, and Jacob—of whom the first is the grandfather of Lawyer Wilson, of this place.

* See Appendix—Note 2.

her back, and thus skated across the noble river Rhine, and
at some one of the neighboring ports, secured a passage to
New York. In this country, but under what auspices, has
not been positively ascertained; he was educated for the
ministry, probably under Dorsius, of Pennsylvania. In
September, 1771, he was called to a German Reformed
church * at Germantown, in this State, which congregation
was under the care of the German Coetus. A couple of
years before, he had married Miss Margaret Miller, daughter of Sebastian Miller, a merchant of that place.

Mr. Foering only remained at Germantown about eight
months, having been called, on March 21st, 1772, to the
German Reformed church in the city of New York. He
succeeded Rev. Mr. Kern, who had been laboring there for
eight years, and at the same time transferred his relations
to the Dutch Coetus. In that place he preached twice
every Sabbath in German, and on Wednesday evenings in
English. He was able also to preach in the Dutch tongue.
But his stay in New York was not very long. In eighteen
months after his settlement, he received his first call to New
Millstone, and eleven months later the second call, which
he accepted. His congregation in New York were very
loathe to part with him, because of his fidelity and zeal.
But when he at length felt it his duty to remove, his church
sent a letter to the Consistory here, warmly commending
him to their love and care, hoping that he would win many
souls to Christ, and that he would dwell and prosper
among them, until his Lord should call him to his ever-
lasting rest. This was, indeed, literally fulfilled. As he

* Which one of the early Germantowns this is, I do not know. It
was a German Reformed, and not a Lutheran church, as the call, still
preserved, shows.

left them, his congregation presented him with a service of silver, in token of their regard, and which is used by his descendants, and the descendants of his wife by a second marriage, now living in Philadelphia, to the present day.

Mr. Foering was a man of deep personal piety. He had been called to New York, as his call, (still preserved,) expressly states, upon the recommendation of Rev. Mr. Weyburgh, *because he was a man who had spirit and life, and who would take trouble to bring souls to the Lord Jesus.* Some scraps of correspondence, which have been preserved in his family, have a peculiar unction of piety about them. He also was the author of several poetic effusions, on religious topics, and of at least one, which has been preserved, said to be descriptive of the lady to whom he was engaged, and whom he afterward married. He was an ardent and active patriot also, in the American Revolution, and one of the original trustees in Queen's College.*

During the first eighteen months of his ministry here, which brings us down to the Declaration of Independence, eighteen persons united with the church on profession of their faith. During the next three years, down to his death, not a single one. The excitement and the party strife, and the frequent proximity of the armies, seriously interfered even with the religious services.

---

* During his ministry here, (April 6th, 1775,) the church was incorporated under the name of Hillsborough, (the name of the township,) to distinguish it from the church at Harlingen, which was then called Millstone. Our township may have taken its name from the Nechanic mountain, within its bounds, or possibly from Lord Hillsborough, though it is not known that he had any interest in these immediate localities. (*Doc. Hist. New York,* vol. i., pp. 354, 499, etc.) All the deeds of church property were now made out anew to the Consistory.

The Consistory of the church well understood the questions and principles involved in the approaching conflict, and six months before the Declaration of Independence, recorded their sentiments upon the records of the church. They called the brewing strife, " an unhappy and unnatural dispute between the ill-disposed ministry of Great Britain, and the oppressed colonies ;" they mourned over the many sins and iniquities of the whole empire ; and set apart one day a month, in which the congregation should come together for humiliation and prayer.*

The manœuverings of the contending armies, in liberty's conflict, frequently involved the quiet and peace of the Millstone valley. In Washington's retreat across the State, in the fall of 1776, he passed within a few miles east of us, along the road from New Brunswick to Princeton, and through Six Mile Run. The first winter of the war, to the no little discouragement of many, the enemy held our State. The main British army was at New Brunswick, and the Hessian mercenaries were roaming through all the country, acting like Goths and Vandals, plundering and outraging the inhabitants. But in January, 1777, having recently captured Trenton and Princeton, Washington marched his forces through our township, on his way to Morristown. It was on this march, or possibly on a similar one in December of the same year, as the army of liberty passed the parsonage, half clothed, unshod, and in want of food, that the patriotic Foering, collecting all the stores of his house, (it being, moreover, just after baking time,) and cutting the food into convenient portions, distributed them, as far as they would go, to the weary and hungry soldiers,

---

* July 17th, 1776, New Jersey answers the letter of the provisional Congress, promising to stand with the others for Independence.

as they hurried on their way. On one of these occasions, as the army passed, they encamped for the night on the field directly south of the present parsonage, Washington himself sleeping in the north-west corner of the parlor of the present homestead of John Van Doren.

On Jan. 20th, 1777, a skirmish took place on the bridge at Weston. An American party had destroyed the boats ascending the Raritan,* laden with provisions, for the British at New Brunswick. They accordingly sent out a foraging party to collect supplies from the country. The Americans met them at this bridge, and attempted to cross, but could not, as the enemy had three field pieces. They numbered six hundred, and had a large number of cattle and a quantity of forage. The Americans numbered four hundred and fifty men, and were under the command of Gen. Dickinson. They therefore sought a ford below, and breaking through the ice, waded the river, flanked the enemy, and routed them, capturing 43 baggage wagons, 104 horses, 118 cattle, 60 or 70 sheep, and made 12 prisoners. They lost five men in this effort, while the enemy lost about thirty. Washington warmly commended Gen. Dickinson for his gallant success. Raids up the Raritan at this time were common.

In the spring of the same year, Washington encamped his men at Middlebrook, near Chimney Rock, 8,000 in number, where he remained for some weeks. The British forces under Howe approached him here, in two columns, Gen. De Heyster halting at Middlebush, and Lord Cornwallis, proceeding to Millstone, encamping on the present farm of Mr. John Wyckoff, on the east side of the river, and both columns fortifying themselves. Millstone was at this time plundered by the British, (June, 1777,) the Pres-

* *Whitehead's Amboy*, p. 340.

byterian and Dutch churches both set on fire,* and the interior at least of the Dutch, completely demolished, though the building was saved. Several farm houses were also burned. But the British, finding Washington's position too strong for them, retired to New Brunswick, and soon evacuated the State, through Amboy and Staten Island, Washington holding Newark and Elizabeth. Previous to this advance of the British, Millstone had been, for at least the six months preceding, in the American lines. This portion of the State was, after the spring of 1777, left comparatively free, for a year and a half. But the church was not effectually repaired till 1784, five years after. Yet religious services were held frequently, somewhere, as the records show that upwards of one hundred infants were baptized during these five years, and also before the church was effectually repaired, no less than forty-two persons professed the faith, though these were under Do. Foering's successor (1780–1784).

In the fall of 1778, after the battle of Freehold, Washington took up his winter-quarters again at Middlebrook. About this time Mr. Foering preached a very patriotic sermon, so as to lead to the formation of a company, from his congregation. The British sent out a party to capture him, so as to prevent his efforts among his people. But his wife received word, in some way, of their intentions, and he being sick in bed, she quickly despatched some of the men-servants to a safe place with a wagon load of goods, and

---

* " On June 24, (1777,) Gen. Howe's army made a movement, and advanced as far as Somerset, a small town lying on the Rarington, betwixt Boundbroock and Princetown, which they plundered, and set fire to two small churches, and several farm houses adjacent; etc."

Narrative of Serjeant Grant.

Col. Hist. N. Y., viii., pp. 728–730.

helping her husband to prepare for his flight, she next, with the terrified maid, geared up the horse herself; and he, though hardly able to proceed, after bidding his wife a sad farewell, started for a place of safety, probably to Washington's camp, and his wife returned into the house to her three children, the oldest but eight years of age. "In a very short time the enemy came up, and in their angry search for one whom with oaths they stigmatized as 'That rebel Foering,' thrust their swords through every bed in the house."

Millstone was during a part of this winter (1778-9) again in the British lines. Several officers were quartered on the Parsonage. "With the exception of one petty subordinate, they all treated their compulsory hostess, with the utmost courtesy and respect. Every day after dinner, they gave her little son a glass of wine, to carry to his mother, with a message to drink Gen. Washington's health. But day by day, as she received it, she poured it into a demijohn, reserving it for her absent and sick husband, whom, she believed, in his feeble health, it would greatly benefit. Upon the departure of her guests, by the evacuation of the neighborhood, by the British, and her husband's return, greatly enfeebled in health, she told him she had a treat for him. But to her consternation, when she took down the demijohn, it was empty. An Irish woman in her employ had drank it all." *

An anecdote is still preserved in the family, of Mrs. Foering's patriotism and courage. "In the dark days of the occupancy of the British, they made frequent levies upon the parsonage for butter, even after they had stolen all the cows they could lay their hands on. Mrs. Foering requested the girl, (Katy Davis, mother of our late member

* Extract from letter of Miss Sarah C. Souder.

Ab. Davis,) to hide it, when she knew of their approach.
A couple of British soldiers soon came with their usual
demand. Mrs. Foering replied that she had no butter
for them, (her veracity depending on the emphasis.) 'A
likely story, indeed,' they said, 'that such a fine place
is without butter.' 'How can you expect butter,' exclaimed
she, ' when you have already taken away my cows ?' Just
then, Katy Davis came into the room, not knowing of the
soldiers' presence, with a great pewter dish of butter, fresh
from the churn, exclaiming, 'Where shall I hide it? what
shall I do with it?' 'Do with it,' exclaimed Mrs. Foering,
' why throw it to the hogs, sooner than let them have it.'
Seizing the butter from the terrified maid, she gave it a
sling across the kitchen, and over the oven, behind which
it lodged out of sight of the men, and as they supposed, out
of reach. Exasperated as they were, they did not injure
her, and after the men were gone, the butter was recovered." * This was just before her husband's return.

Mr. Foering leaving home sick, and subjected to exposure
in his flight, took a heavy cold, from which consumption
resulted, and he soon died. The day before his death, he
baptized an infant son, five days old. His mother proposed
naming her son Jacob, after her brother. No, replied Mr.
Foering, Jacob was a deceiver. Let him be called Abraham,† who was faithful! So after the "Friend of God"

* Extract from a letter of Miss Sarah C. Souder.
† Mr. Foering left four sons, Samuel, John, Frederick, and Abraham
P. Mrs. Laudenslager, of Philadelphia, is a daughter of Abraham, and
Mrs. Read, her daughter, contributed a valuable letter concerning her
ancestor. Mr. Foering's widow, afterward married Dr. Janus, of
Philadelphia, and she was again left a widow in 1796. She died in
1823. Miss Sarah C. Souder, her grand-daughter by this second marriage, has contributed a number of valuable papers and letters, which
have greatly aided in the preparation of this discourse.

the child was named, and it is said, he well deserved it
This was the last official act of an earnest, holy, patriotic
life. The next day, being March 29th, 1779, the first pastor
of this church breathed his last. His body was deposited
under the church, in front of the sacred desk, whence had
issued the kindred lessons of religion and liberty, and his
dust yet reposes beneath us, in this second edifice, to this
day.*

His wife, after his death, being administratrix in connection with her father, at once loaned the struggling government, in good currency, the sum of $400. Her patriotism
did not die with her husband.

Rev. Cor. T. Demarest describes Mr. Foering as a gentle-
man of the German Calvinistic Church, of orthodox sentiments, and of true piety. Three weeks before his death,
the Consistory, notwithstanding the lamentable times, raised
the sum of £472, or $1190, for the last payment on the par-
sonage. (March 6, 1779.)

In the fall of the same year, the Court House in this village was burned. It stood on the lot now partly occupied
by Miss Mary Suydam. Its destruction was connected with
the successful efforts of the British, to defeat Washington's
plan for the capture of New York. For this purpose he
secretly built fifty flat boats, on the Delaware, capable of
holding seventy men each, and, putting them on wheels,
rolled them across the State, to Van Veghten's Bridge, over
the Raritan, (near Harmony Plains.) Some of the older people still remember their parents' accounts of these strange
wheeled craft, passing through this place. In these he intended ultimately to cross the Hudson with his men. Lt.
Col. Simcoe of the Queen's rangers, offered himself for the

---

* By a receipt still preserved, it appears that he once paid £120 for
a negro boy by the name of Frank,—bought of Ab. Quilp.

dangerous task of burning these boats, and defeating Washington's design. His superior officers approved the plan,
and he undertook it. The Americans were all absent from
the locality to be traversed, only the militia being left. His
plan was to ride from Amboy, keeping back from the river,
on the North side of the Raritan, get to the boats before
day-light and burn them, and avoiding New Brunswick by
keeping to the west of it, to reappear on the Raritan below
Brunswick, at the South River, where he was to meet another party of the British under Major Armstrong, and try
and decoy the by this time pursuing Americans into an
ambuscade.

They started on October 25th, with eighty troopers from
Staten Island, but were delayed in crossing, and were not
ready to leave Amboy till day-break the next morning.
Still they proceeded. They feigned to be Americans, and
accosted the people pleasantly as they passed. But Simcoe
was recognized when a little East of Bound Brook, and
word was instantly sent to Gov. Livingston at New Brunswick, to prepare to head them off. They tried to burn
Washington's huts at Middlebrook, but did not succeed.
They reached the bridge and found eighteen of the boats,
and spent forty minutes in firing them. They went to the
Raritan Dutch Church standing close by, which contained
harness and provision stores, and fired it, making the
Commissary and his men prisoners. A shot was now fired
at the party from the opposite bank, but they at once cross-
ed, and came up to Millstone, to the Court House here.
Simcoe lamented that they had been delayed in starting,
as it was now late, and the country was becoming alarmed
and beginning to assemble about him. He found three
tories as prisoners in the court-house: one of them (he says
was chained to the floor and was a dreadful spectacle, being
almost starved. These were liberated, and the soldiers asked

permission to burn the court-house, which, since it was un-
connected with any other building, was granted. But it was
an unfortunate circumstance for Simcoe, as the light showed
his enemies his position; alarm guns were fired in every
direction, and Gov. Livingston notified to judge of the enemy's whereabouts, by these shots. The party passed down
through Middlebush, threatening the inhabitants that if the
firing in the rear were not discontinued, they would burn
their houses; but as they approached New Brunswick, intending to turn south-ward and leave that city on their left,
at the road a couple of miles this side, but which they miss-
ed, they fell into an ambuscade of Americans, Simcoe's horse
being shot under him, and himself and some of his men
being made prisoners. He remained a prisoner a couple
of months at Burlington.* An American Captain, by the
name of Voorheese, was killed. There were but few events
of general interest, after this, in this vicinity, during the
war.

The congregation knew not where to look for another
minister in those troublous times, and were reduced to their
former circumstances, of depending upon the neighboring
churches, when unexpectedly a refugee preacher arrived in
the midst of them.

Solomon Froeligh had been born at Red Hook, near Albany, on May 29th, 1750, O. S. In his fourteenth year, his
mind was deeply impressed with religious convictions, he
being then under the pastoral care of Rev. John Schenema,
the minister of Catskill and Coxsackie. His father was a
farmer. Young Solomon begged his parents to give him a
liberal education, but their circumstances hardly permitted
it. But at length, through his mother's influence, when in
his 18th year, he was placed under the care of Rev. Dirck

* Whitehead's Amboy, p. 353.

Romeyn, the pastor of Marbletown, Warwarsing and Rochester, to begin the study of Latin and Greek. He never received any assistance from his father, but assisted himself by teaching school. Soon after, to possess better privileges, he removed to Hackensack, and entered there the celebrated academy of Dr. Peter Wilson. Here he made such progress that Princeton College conferred on him the degree of A. B. About the same time (Nov. 11, 1771,) he married Rachel Vanderbeck. He now proceeded to the study of theology, under Rev. John H. Goetschius, formerly of Switzerland, but now preaching at Hackensack. He was licensed to preach the Gospel Oct. 1st, 1774, and on June 11th, 1775, was ordained pastor of the four united churches of Long Island, it being only a year before the breaking out of the Revolution.

With his ardent nature he could not help taking sides in that great struggle. The district in which he lived was noted also for its disaffection to the cause of Independence. Yet in the midst of enemies, he labored and prayed boldly for his country's freedom.*

Shortly after the battle of Long Island in August 1776, and which occurred in the territory of his congregations, he found it necessary to flee to save his life, narrowly escaping. He fled to Jamaica, and Newtown, and having been concealed one night in the house of Mr. Rapalje at Hurl-gate, he was put across the river to Harlem. He went first to Hackensack, and preached while there a most patriotic sermon from 2 Chron. 11 : 4, exhorting the inhabitants not to fight against the cause of Independence, to which many there were inclined. Dr. Laidlie, the colleague of Dr. Livingston, heard him, and warmly commended him. In his flight he lost his cattle, furniture, books, and clothing, indeed every

* Riken's Annals of Newtown, p. 199, and pamphlets on the secession.

thing. In company with Dr. Livingston, both being on
horseback, he started for Poughkeepsie, keeping on the
west-side of the Hudson, and for three years he supplied the
pulpits of **Fishkill and Poughkeepsie** (1776–1779). But
in 1799, he left them, probably on account of the campaigns,
then beginning in that vicinity.

In the spring of 1780, he appeared in **Millstone, one year
after** Mr. Foering's death, and the Consistory at once appointed Mr. Ernestus Van Harlingen to wait upon him and
try and secure his services, till he could return to his
churches on Long Island. They offered to give him as salary
268 bushels of wheat a year, each bushel to weigh 60
pounds.

He declined entering into a temporary arrangement, but
said he would accept a call, which the Consistory gladly
offered to give him, and he moved into the parsonage, June
5th, 1780. The Consistory paid his expenses of moving,
which **in the money of the day, amounted to $1455, one**
dollar in gold **being worth at the time $40 of the Continen-**
tal currency.

But it was impossible for him to get a formal dismission
from his churches on Long Island, as the enemy held both
the Island and the city. But the Synod, meeting in October 1780, at New Paltz, appointed a **committee** to settle a
question of dispute between our congregation and the three
neighboring congregations, in respect to the bounds of each,
and if they succeeded in effecting amity, they were then
empowered **in the name of the Synod, to approve the call,**
and in this very unusual case to dismiss him from his congregations on Long Island.

But during the summer of 1780, and before the call was
acted on from this congregation, Nechanic* sought to unite

* In 1775 (November 13th) we find an order from the Consistory of

with us, and secure a part of Mr. Froeligh's services, Nechanic and Sourland being then under the care of Rev. John M. Van Harlingen. Articles of agreement were entered into, and Mr. Froeligh's call, as finally approved, stands in the name of the two churches, and is dated Sept. 4, 1780.* He was to preach two Sundays out of three, at Millstone, and one at Nechanic, and was to alternate between the Dutch and English. At Nechanic, when the days were long, he was to preach twice a day. Millstone was to furnish one hundred and sixty bushels of good winter wheat, and Nechanic one hundred and eight. In 1784 (April 12,) by mutual consent, his salary was changed to £120 proclamation money, of which Nechanic paid £40, and Millstone £80 a year.

The next year, October 1st, 1782, the Synod met in the church of New Millstone. New York was their general place of meeting, both before and after the war, but during the war their meetings were held at places remote from the scene of hostilities, and in 1782, our defaced and desolated church, almost unfit to be occupied, welcomed the Synod of the denomination within its blackened walls. The Rev. Harmanus Meyer, the pastor at Paterson and Pompton Plains, presided over the body, which consisted, however, of only nine members. Rev. Dr. Dirck Romeyn preached the opening sermon, from Isaiah iv. 5: "And the Lord will create *upon every dwelling place of Mount Zion, and upon all her assemblies,* a cloud and smoke by day, and the

Millstone to the Consistory of Nechanic, given to Mr. Foering, for £5 15s. 11d., on account of his salary. Possibly some arrangement between Mr. Foering and Nechanic may have temporarily existed.

* The dates on the call, and the statements in the Mints. of Gen. Synod, vol. i., pp. 80–97, do not altogether agree. I follow the official documents in possession of this church.

shining of a flaming fire by night, for above all, the glory shall be a defence," a grand text from which to draw encouragement and consolation for the people of God, in those troublous times. For He was indeed ever present with them and their cause, as He had been visibly present to Israel in the cloud and fire. It was at this meeting that Simeon Van Arsdale was examined and afterward licensed, and who settled at Readington soon after, and died in early life, (1783–1787.)

The war now being over, and no further dangers being apprehended, the Consistory felt the necessity of effectually repairing the church.* But they had suffered so much from the raids and depredations of the enemy, that they were really unable to go to the necessary expense. There had been an almost constant accession of immigrants from Long Island to this county, from among the Dutch, up to the beginning of the war. The ties of relationship were not yet forgotten, and undoubtedly frequent visitations back and forth, when the state of the country did not forbid, were made. Mr. Froeligh, moreover, had labored among the immediate relatives of the people here, when he had been settled on Long Island, and in fact this people was a colony from his former charges, though before his settlement over them. They therefore appointed a committee, consisting of Mr. Froeligh, Capt. Cornelius Lott, and Peter Ditmarse, to visit Long Island, and solicit help, as the congregations there had suffered very little, they having been in the British lines throughout the war. The subscription states that our church had been much distressed, the inhabitants plundered, and the church building in part destroyed, and rendered useless; that the people were unable to bear all

---

* It appears that in 1779, Cor. Cornell had given £137 for repairing the church, and another individual (name unknown) £91.

the expense required alone, and hence were under the *disagreeable necessity* of appealing for help to those whom Providence had smiled on more kindly, hoping that from sympathy, they would be induced to charity and benevolence toward us. The subscription also states, that the names of such as gave should be handed down to posterity on the records of the church.* This has been done. They secured thus, on Long Island, the sum of £85, or about $212, and the church was now repaired and rendered again comfortable. The seats were now also sold, by which $100 were raised in addition, and thus the repairs paid for.

While on Long Island, soliciting funds, Mr. Froeligh's old charges tried hard to keep him there, as he had never been regularly dismissed.† But he said he was now united to another, and refused to remain. He labored here about six years. He was greatly encouraged at the beginning of his ministry, by a large accession to the church. This is, indeed, the more remarkable, as the times of the Revolution are noted for their profligacy and immorality. The first winter that he was here, he received fourteen on profession, and three by certificate. The next fall, he received sixteen by profession, and two by certificate, but during the rest of his ministry only six. The revivals under him occurred while they had no respectable place of worship. Mr. Froeligh's life and experience were somewhat peculiar. His spiritual exercises were very deep and overpowering. He says of himself in a letter, " While preaching at Millstone and Nechanic, I experienced God's smiles and his frowns. Here I have been both on the mount and in the valley. The neighboring ministers opposed my settlement, and I was not installed for a whole year. I had officiated but a short time in these congregations, when to my great

* See Appendix—Note 3.   † *Riker's Annals*, p. 241.

joy, a general awakening broke out among my people. It affected persons of every age and color. The word preached became powerful; many became solicitous inquirers what they should do to be saved; many of profligate morals became professing and praying Christians. This unexpected season filled my heart with great delight, as I began to despair that God would ever own me by His blessing on my labors. But alas! I was too much elated. I imputed too much to my own abilities, and did not give God all the glory. Therefore my joy was changed into sorrow. I was seized with a dangerous illness, and brought to the gates of death. I cannot say that my confidence in the redemption of Christ was much shaken during my illness, and it pleased the Lord to restore me. But soon after he gave me up to the most gloomy despair, in which I continued for six years; sometimes sunk into inexpressible blackness of despondency, overwhelmed with sadness, bereaved of all satisfaction, haunted by shocking fears of misery, and assaulted by the most horrid temptations to deism, of which I had never experienced the least before. My situation was frequently rendered intolerable by sudden injections of Satan's fiery darts. The arch-fiend so far succeeded, that I thought I could not preach, and did actually desist for several weeks; but it pleased the Lord to show me that it was a delusion, and I again betook myself to the work, and was enabled to preach with more accuracy than I had anticipated. The Lord was pleased to deliver me out of this horrible pit, and out of the miry clay; since which I have uniformly enjoyed considerable peace and tranquillity of mind." *

In 1786 he received a call to the two congregations of Hackensack and Schráalenberg, which he accepted, and in

* This letter was written in his old age, nearly forty years afterward.

which places he continued to labor till his death, which occurred October 8th, 1827. With his life subsequent to his departure from us, we have but little to do. In 1791 he was elected Professor of Theology, in place of Dr. Meyer, of Pompton, who had died. In his new field, he found his churches divided into two parties, with two Consistories, on account of a difficulty which had begun fifty years before, and having tried to unite them, and failing, he took sides with the party which were very strenuous in doctrine, and opposed to the commingling of Christians of different names, virtually exalting doctrine above practical religion, and refusing to unite in the great efforts of Christian union and fraternization, under the power of which the Bible and Tract and Missionary, and other union Societies, were organized, until at last himself and four others seceded from the Dutch church in 1822, when he was seventy-two years of age, thirty-six years after his departure from Millstone. He was accordingly deposed from the professorship and the ministry by General Synod, and although the True Reformed Dutch church which he organized continued to increase, for six years quite rapidly,* since that time it has been steadily declining, and but few congregations of any strength remain. Yet the division caused an incalculable amount of bad feeling and of sin in Bergen county, and some other places.

With his departure from this place, the union between Nechanic and Millstone ended, (June 8, 1786,) and Rev. Mr. Leydt, of New Brunswick and Six Mile Run, having died in 1783,† that union was also dissolved, and now Six

---

* The Seceder church culminated in 1830, when they had thirty congregations.

† He died June 2d, aged sixty-five. His tombstone yet remains at Three Mile Run. His wife, Treyntje Sleght Egugnoort, died December

Mile Run and Millstone enter into an agreement to call a minister together. They agree to pay £130 in equal parts, and to have equal services. In Millstone one-half the preaching was to be in Dutch, and one-half in English, while in Six Mile Run two-thirds to be in Dutch and one-third in English. Indeed these two congregations made a formal call to retain Mr. Froeligh, when he contemplated removing to Hackensack, but without success.

In the meantime, during the vacancy, John M. Van Har-lingen, the son of Ernestus Van Harlingen, of this place, and nephew of the old pastor of the same name at Sourland, was examined by Synod in New York, (October, 1786,) and licensed to preach the Gospel; and on May 1st, 1787, the call of the two churches upon him was approved by Synod. He was ordained during the summer. His own father was one of his elders.

John M. Van Harlingen labored in these churches about eight years. It was during his ministry, that the title and incorporation of the church were finally fixed. Immediately after the Revolution, (1784,) they took measures to have their old English charter confirmed by the General Assembly of the State of New Jersey, and to have all their former legal acts ratified. This was secured on the condition that the allegiance required in the charter to the king, should henceforth be given to the State of New Jersey, (the union of the States not yet existing.) This was under Froeligh But in 1790, all the neighboring churches, whether collegiate or single, including our own, repudiated their old charters, that they might incorporate, according to the new law of 1789. In 1790, therefore, the Consistory became

2d, 1763, aged thirty-six. His daughter, Elizabeth, died October 27th, 1760, aged twelve, and Anne, died June 10th, 1760, aged seven months.

incorporated under the laws of the United States and the State of New Jersey, by the name of "The New Corporation of the Minister, Elders, and Deacons, of the Congregation of Hillsborough." Six Mile Run being freed from the common charter of the five churches obtained in 1753, by the mutual relinquishment of the same in 1790, also became incorporated by herself this year. The union between our own church and theirs was ecclesiastical simply, but not corporate.

But each of the churches had a parsonage, and in reference to this, they agreed that Mr. Van Harlingen should live in the parsonage at Millstone on the hill, and that Six Mile Run should sell theirs, (it belonging equally to the church of New Brunswick,) and that half the money they received, should be paid to Millstone, which should be considered a full compensation. Accordingly, they sold their parsonage property to Mr. Jacob Skillman, for £390 16s. 8d., (proclamation money,) and paid £195 8s. 4d. (or $488) to Millstone. It was situated about a mile and a half east of Six Mile Run Church, on the New Brunswick road. Here Dominie Leydt had lived for thirty-five years, and before him, near the same place, the first Frelinghuysen.

The Dutch language was now rapidly losing ground. Although used to a great extent as the language of the household, yet the theological and biblical expressions, owing to English education, were better understood in English. While twenty years before, Dominie Foering had been called to preach at Millstone, wholly in English, yet under Froeligh and Van Harlingen, the arrangement was changed, out of deference to the older people. The day after Christmas, however, in 1791, Consistory resolved that the services on the holidays, which do not fall on Sabbath days, shall henceforth be performed wholly in English.

Mr. Van Harlingen's ministry, if we may judge from the additions to the church, was successful. Thirty-four united with the church during the first five years of his ministry, two of these by certificate. During the last three, not one. We have seen before the same process of additions at first in the ministry of each of his predecessors. The first few years they were blessed ; during the last years of their ministry, no visible fruits appear.

Mr. Van Harlingen, for reasons not stated,* resigned in the summer of 1795, but continued to live in this village. He was a man of extensive acquisitions, and in June, 1812, when the plan of the Theological school was fully organized, such confidence was had in his abilities, that he was elected by the General Synod, Professor of Hebrew and Ecclesiastical History, in place of Dr. Bassett, of Albany, who had just resigned. He was thus associated with Dr. Livingston and Rev. Sol. Froeligh. Dr. Livingston taught in New Brunswick. The other two were expected to teach at their own homes, as Dr. Froeligh had already been doing for twenty-one years. Mr. Van Harlingen was the translator of the English version of Vanderkemp on the Heidelbergh Catechism.

But his services in his new field were of short duration. The Master called him to his rest in about a year from his appointment. He died, June 16th, 1813, in the fifty-second year of his age.† His remains lie in the adjacent church-yard, awaiting the resurrection of the just.

After the resignation of Mr. Van Harlingen, (1796,) this

* His last text, as pastor here, is said to have been Jer. xx. 10.

† The Classis have recorded a lamentation, in their minutes, that since Dos. Condict and Van Harlingen have died, strict examinations of students must cease. (Vol. ii., p. 66.) Surely not very complimentary to the survivors !

church first called Rev. Peter Lowe, who had been examined
and licensed at the same time as Mr. Van Harlingen, and
who was now laboring in the former charges of Mr.
Froeligh, on Long Island.   But he did not accept the call.
But among the members of Classis who supplied the pulpit
during the vacancy, appeared a young man from the Classis
of Hackensack, in September and November, 1796, and in
March, 1797, and with whom the people were well pleased.
This was James Spencer Cannon.   Six Mile Run again
united with Millstone in the call, and he was ordained and
installed at Millstone, May 1st, 1797.

He writes in the church record in his own hand, the date
of his ordination, and adds concerning himself: " To whom,
therefore, this church register book is committed, to pre-
serve inviolate, and to transmit to posterity the acts and
proceedings of the Dutch Reformed Congregation of Hillsborough, under my ministry among them."

He was born in the island of Curaçoa, (one of the West
Indies,) Jan. 28th, 1776.   His father was of Irish descent,
his mother of New England.   Their home was in the city
of New York, when not on the sea.   James was sent to
school to Dr. Peter Wilson at Hackensack, and in a few
years his father was lost at sea.   He completed his acade-
mical education under Dr. Miller, Dr. Wilson's successor.

In 1794, he professed religion, under Dr. Solomon Froeligh at Hackensack, under whom he studied theology also
till the spring of 1796, completing his course under Dr.
Livingston, then on Long Island, and was, during that season, licensed by the Classis of Hackensack, in company with
Peter Labagh.   After considering several calls which were
made upon him, he settled over this and the neighboring
church of Six Mile Run, at the time already stated   During the vacancy, and intending to continue united with Six

Mile Run, the Consistory here sold their parsonage property, to Martin Shenck, for £400, proclamation money, to be paid in four equal payments; £200 of this they paid to Six Mile Run. On the first of May of the same year, the two churches purchased a house and lot of land, containing twenty-two acres, about a mile west of Six Mile Run Church, and five acres of woodland near the Six Mile Run Church, on the same road, and fourteen acres of woodland on sand hills, in the Swamp, (of Cor. Barcaloo,) paying for all £624. Dr. Cannon lived in the parsonage provided, a few years, when it was sold, and the use of the money allowed him, while he himself bought a place at Pleasant Plains, where he continued to reside until his removal to New Brunswick.

But we have now come down to the opening of the present century, and what wonderful changes have taken place! A century before, an almost unbroken wilderness, but now covered with enterprising farmers and artisans, and nine Dutch churches, not to speak of many others, in a circumference of twenty miles diameter. Raritan, the oldest church, had seen Hardenberg dismissed to the North, (to the churches of Marbletown and Rochester) in 1781, who five years later returned to this section to take charge of the church of New Brunswick, and to preside over the College. In 1793, the Lord took him home, and Dr. Ira Condict succeeded him there, for 18 years. Theodore Frelinghuysen Romeyn* had succeeded Hardenberg at Raritan, and in less than a year and-a-half, death called him away, at the early age of 25, (1784–1785;) and he had been succeeded by Rev. John Duryee in 1786, who labored at Somerville for thirteen years, when, having taken charge of Bedminster and Whitehouse for a couple of years, he removed to Fairfield

* Son of Rev. Thos. Romeyn, who had married Margaret Frelinghuysen.

in Passaic County, where he died about thirty years ago; and
at the opening of the century the excellent Vredenburgh
had begun his labors at Somerville, and whose wondrous
fruits appeared after his death.   Old Dr. Studdiford with his
forty years of service, (1787–1826,) yet remembered by many,
had succeeded the short ministry of Van Arsdale at Readington, (1783–1787,) who like the second Frelinghuysen
and Romeyn in the same localities had so early been called
to rest.   Old Dominie Van Harlingen, who gave name to
one of his congregations after his death, a native originally
of our own village, and a brother of our active elder Ernestus, having labored for a generation (1761–1795,) in Father
Ludlow's and Brother Gardner's churches, preaching only
in the Dutch, and having for a time at Nechanic a colleague
in our own Froeligh received a year or two before his death,
(1794,) an English colleague, in Rev. Wm. R. Smith, the
brother of President Smith of Princeton College.   And he
in turn, after burying his venerable father in the ministry
in 1795, received three years later the Rev. Henry Polhemus, as his colleague, a native of Harlingen, who labored
with him for ten years.   So that in the year 1800 we have
laboring in the Dutch churches of the Raritan and its
branches, and as companions of the yet youthful and afterward eminent Cannon, the sainted Vredenburgh and Studdiford, Polhemus and Smith, Duryee and Condict, and Van
Harlingen without charge in this village, and an attendant
on young Cannon's ministry.   Here were nine Dutch
churches, and eight ministers, (seven settled,) where a little
more than a-half century before, there had been but one
ambassador of Christ to cultivate this extended field.*

* See appendix, Note 4, where the main data of the history of these
and the later Dutch churches of the Raritan Valley are carried down to the
present time.

The old church in this year again received a thorough repairing, and the seats were taxed to defray the expenses. Four years later the music of a church bell first resounded over these fields. It was made to order, in New Haven, and cost £16.12s. and 9d, or a little more than $40, and about $20 more for transportation. But Mr. Cannon's field, with the increase of population, was becoming too large for one man. Each of the churches also began to feel able to support a preacher alone. He lived moreover remote from Millstone, which often proved very inconvenient. These, and other reasons not necessary to be specified, induced Mr. Cannon early in 1807, after ten years of labor, to resign his call to Millstone, and our ecclesiastical relation with Six Mile Run was at the same time dissolved, the latter church calling Mr. Cannon alone. He has left a list of the actual number of communicants for the year 1801, whence it appears that this church then had seventy members. But another list in his own hand in 1806,* reports only fifty-five, not one-fifth the present number. He received during the first six and-a-half years of his ministry here, thirty-seven on profession, and sixteen by certificate. During the last year and-a-half, none. He was eminently a pastor, as his excellent work on Pastoral Theology, adopted in many institutions of our land, abundantly proves. With the close of his ministry among you, ended your collegiate connections with other congregations, about sixty years ago. During the first eight years, being without a pastor, and dependent upon the neighboring ministers for supply; and then after Foering's four and-a-half years ministry here alone, for twenty-seven years you had shared your Sabbath services with Nechanic and Six Mile Run. Henceforth, you deter-

* See appendix, **Note 5**

mined to meet **every Sabbath** in your own sanctuary, to
enjoy the privileges of the Gospel.

Mr. Cannon, after about twenty years of service at Six
Mile Run, was in 1826, elected as Professor of Ecclesiastical
History and **Church Government,** as successor to the lamented Woodhull, in the Seminary at New Brunswick. He
became then colleague of Rev. Dr. John De Witt, (the father
of the present Professor of the same name,) and of Rev. Dr.
Milledoler, the successor of Dr. Livingston. Here for a
quarter of a century he labored for his Master, till He called
him to a higher sphere of duties above. He died on Sabbath, July 25th, 1852.

Rev. John Schureman became the fifth pastor of this
church. He was called on April 20th, 1807, from the
church of Bedminster, and began his duties here soon after.
He was born October 19th, 1778, near New Brunswick.
He graduated from the college in that place in 1795, and
after pursuing his theological studies under Dr. Livingston,
he was licensed to preach in 1800. The next year he settled
at Bedminster, where he remained for six years. He was
probably a descendant of the schoolmaster Schureman, who
came to America in 1719 with Mr. Frelinghuysen, and settled with him at Three Mile Run.

The Consistory, having no parsonage, having sold out
their interest in their last property to Six Mile Run church,
Mr. Schureman lived on the place now occupied by Mr.
Jacob Van Cleeve, near Blackwell's Mills. During his
ministry, an important reformation in the management of
the finances of the church was attempted, and partly succeeded. Many of the pew-holders gave up their old deeds
to the Consistory, and received new ones in return, in
which the pews were made directly assessable for all the
expenses of the church. But his short pastorate here pre-

vented the plan from being carried out fully, and in 1828, at the rebuilding of the church, unfortunately, it was not established. This is now a change eminently desirable, for the interests and character of the church. It should not be longer delayed.

In the fall of 1809 (Nov. 17) the Consistory agreed to his request to dissolve their relations, he having accepted a call to the Collegiate church in New York. During the two years and a half of his ministry here, he received into the church, on profession, seventeen, and by certificate, ten, in all twenty-seven.

Mr. Schureman was not of strong constitution. His health soon failed him in New York, and in two years after he left this church, (viz., in 1811,) he removed to New Brunswick, having been chosen Vice-President of the College, as successor to Dr. Condict.* But the College was at this time almost dead. He received, meanwhile, successive calls from the church of New Brunswick, and in the spring of 1813, was installed as its pastor. But his poor health in three months compelled him to give up this charge. In 1815, the church, realizing his abilities, appointed him Professor of History and Church Government. But in May, 1818, he died. Dr. Livingston writes concerning him : " He was mild and pleasant ; discerning and firm ; steadfast, but not obstinate ; zealous, but not assuming. The frequent hemorrhage of his lungs, and the habitual weakness of his constitution, prevented him from close and intense studies ; yet he was a good Belle-lettres scholar. His style was correct and pure ; and he made such progress in the official branches of his professorship, that his lectures upon ecclesiastical history and pastoral theology were highly

* See *Gunn's Livingston*, p. 289. Dr. Condict died June 1st, 1811.

acceptable and very useful. The suavity of his manners, and the propriety of his conduct, endeared him to the students, and recommended him to the respect and affection of all who knew him. He was growing into extensive usefulness, and had he lived and progressed, as he begun, would have become a treasure to the Theological College."

We have now come down to a time within the memory of many yet living, viz., the beginning of Rev. John L. Zabriskie's ministry, a man who served this church nearly half of its term of existence.

Mr. Zabriskie was of Polish extraction, having descended from Albert Saboroweski, who arrived in this country in the ship Fox, in 1662, settling at once at Hackensack. This Albert had studied for the Lutheran ministry, it is said,* but was in some way impressed into the army, and at length availed himself of an opportunity which offered, to come to this country. He bought a large tract of land of the Indians, called Paramus, where his children mostly settled, and whence the family have spread abroad. Rev. Mr. Zabriskie was the son of John, and of the fourth generation in this country, having been born March 4th, 1779, three weeks before your first pastor's death.

He graduated at Union College in 1798, being a member of the first class in that institution, and was licensed to preach in 1801 by the Classis of Rensselaer. He first settled over the united churches of Greenbush and Wynantskill, succeeding Rev. J. V. C. Romeyn, and where he continued for about eight years. He preached here for the first in the month of February, 1810, and moved to Millstone in May, 1811,† fifty-five years ago, and was installed by Rev. Mr. Cannon.

* *Winfield's Historical Sermon* at Paramus.
† *Minutes of Classis of New Brunswick*, vol. ii., pp. 14 56.

The church at the time of his settlement had not more than about seventy members, and eighty-four families. This may appear strange, since there were about as many signatures to the first petition for a church, nearly half a century before. But it must be remembered that not all of these were allowed to join the new congregation then, and many families had been broken up during the Revolution, and the country much impoverished. The church of Mill-stone was, at the beginning of Mr. Zabriskie's ministry, among the weakest on the Raritan and its branches; while now, as far as members go, and ability, it is among the strongest. His ministry began about the time when the incipient steps were in progress, of all those great union associations of piety, philanthropy, and benevolence, which have since so greatly blessed, and are still blessing, our world. He was among the earliest friends of the New Jersey Bible Society, the first of those *State* societies which, when their numbers had increased, merged themselves into the one grand American Bible Society. It was a grand and hitherto unequalled privilege to begin life with this century, and in this new and freed country, amid all the rapidly developing plans of Providence, for the progress of His church, and the elevation of mankind;—to live in an age when wonder succeeded wonder in the physical, and scientific and moral worlds; and with each succeeding decade, the privileges and blessings and causes of adoration still increasing. It is now a blessed privilege for the Christian to appreciate and help on these works of Providence. It seems to have been Mr. Zabriskie's work to build up this church to strength and numbers through the Spirit's influence, that she might then take an active and important, yea, a prominent part in these great plans of God. Let us not fail, as ancient Israel so often did, to understand our duty.

Shortly after Mr. Zabriskie's settlement here, early in 1812, the Consistory again provided a parsonage property for themselves. They bought the plot* now occupied by Dr. Fred. Blackwell, of Dan. Disborough, for $1,250, and immediate repairs bestowed, swelled this amount to $2,232. But this place was only occupied three or four years, when Mr. Zabriskie purchased a property of his own on the hill, where he resided till his death. And the Consistory sold their parsonage to Dr. Wm. McKissack.

During the first eighteen years of his ministry here, he preached in the old church, reminding them still of early times, of poverty and strife and victory, in freedom's conflict. But it had long been felt that this church was too small for the growing congregation, and repeated efforts had been made to remedy the evil. The building had received a slight repairing during the Revolution, and a more considerable one in 1783, when money had been solicited abroad. Again in 1800, it was very thoroughly renovated, and the pews re-arranged and sold anew to pay expenses. In 1805, they agitated the matter of putting a gallery in the church, to increase the accommodation, but failed of success; and again in 1816, $800 were subscribed for this object, but without result. The old building continued to be occupied till April 22d, 1828, the subject of re-building having been agitated, (says Dominie Zabriskie, in a certain paper,) for twenty-five years, without being able to agree on the best course. But on May 26th, 1827, a memorial was presented to the Consistory, signed by eighty persons,

---

* Beginning at the end of a large flat stone, on the road leading from John Bayard's, to Wm. Blackwell's Mills, on the N. side of a small brook, thence along the road S. 3° W. 1 ch. 38 links, thence N. 87¼° E. along Van Doren's land, 6 ch. 22 links, N. 3° E. 1 ch. 38 links, N. 2¼° W. 3 chains, S. 87¼° W. 6 chains to said road, and along said road to place of beginning, containing 2 4-10 acres.

respectfully requesting the Consistory to call a meeting of the congregation, to devise means for enlarging or rebuilding the church. Frequent meetings were held, and at last the Consistory determined that in conformity with the wishes of a large portion of the congregation, a new church should be erected. $1,000 were allowed to the pew-holders in the old church, to be properly credited between them, to go toward the purchase of pews in the new church, and John Sutphen, Farrington, Barcaloo, and Abraham Beekman were appointed a Committee, to appraise the value of the old pews. The edifice was to be built after the model of the new church at Six Mile Run. They had built their second edifice in the same year that our church had been organized,* (1766,) and now a year or two before, and probably stimulating this congregation to the work, they had built the edifice which they now use. Their second building, and our first, both stood for just sixty years, and the present buildings of both congregations are identical in size, being 70x55 feet.

The building committee consisted of Stephen Garretson, Dan. H. Disborough, and Ab. Beekman, subject to the direction of the Consistory. They contracted with Joachim G. Quick for $5,000, including the old church material. Extra expenses accrued, amounting to $317. The corner stone was laid on June 8th, 1828, and an address delivered by the Pastor from Gen. xxviii : 22. "And this stone which I have set for a pillar, shall be God's house ; and of all that Thou shalt give me, I will surely give the tenth unto Thee,"—important and suggestive words. Prayer was also offered for God's blessing on the undertaking. A committee was then appointed, consisting of James B. Elmendorf, Ab. Staats, and John Sutphen, to appraize the pews, the aggregate sum to amount to $6,500. The church was dedicated

---

* Early records at New Brunswick.

on Christmas Sabbath, 1828, the pastor preaching from Ex. xx: 24, "An altar of earth thou shalt make unto Me, and shalt sacrifice thereon thy burnt offerings and thy peace offerings, thy sheep, and thine oxen; in all places where I record My name, I will come unto thee, and I will bless thee." The following Thursday the pews were sold, and $7689 were realized, leaving a considerable surplus in the hands of Consistory.

Mr. Zabriskie's ministry had been quite successful respecting additions to the church, during the time that they worshiped in the old building. Up to the year they demolished their house, he had received 210 members,* of whom 166, had been on profession of their faith. In this same year, (1827) he reports 100 families, and about 200 communicants. The membership had therefore more than doubled during his ministry in the old edifice. But they had now built a large and spacious house, much larger than many supposed to be necessary, and the Lord soon filled it. They had made room for a blessing, and it came. God rewarded, as He ever will, their largeness of spirit, and liberality to Zion. Thirty new families are at once found reported as attendants, and in 1831, the Spirit of grace was most richly poured out on this congregation.† There had been a considerable number of accessions in certain former years; in 1822, and in 1823, twenty-five and fifteen respectively professed the faith; in 1817 and 1818, twenty-eight and sixteen respectively had acknowledged Christ before men; but at this time it averaged nearly one out of every family. In the fall of 1831, 108 were received at a single communion,

---

* We have the names of only 197, but in a report to Classis for 1813, he states that he had received since his settlement here thirteen on profession.

† The revival of this year was universal through the country.

by far the greater proportion of whom are no longer with us. It was indeed a rich blessing from heaven, such as we might again well desire. It remains on record as God's testimony to us, of His fidelity to His promises, and of His love. And let us never forget that by repentance and faith and prayer, He may show us even greater things than these, that we may marvel. On three subsequent occasions, under Father Zabriskie's ministry, viz. in 1837, 1838, and 1843, he received respectively, nineteen, seventeen, and twenty-five, in single years. During his whole ministry in the new church of twenty-two years, he received 280 on profession of faith, and 118 by certificates from other churches, and during his whole pastorate of forty years, the total number received were 446 by profession, and 162 by certificate, or 608 in all. His last report to Classis in the spring of 1850, makes the church membership to be then 291, and 176 families.* The congregation was indeed built up to great strength in numbers during his long pastorate here. The membership had nearly trebled, the families had increased by three-fourths. What a power for good might such an army of Christ become if directing their energies into great, Christian, philanthropic, world-wide, yea divine efforts! This is indeed what our Lord Jesus Christ, who has redeemed us by His own blood, now calls upon us to do.

Father Zabriskie died August 15th, 1850, at the age of 71 years. His dust lies in the adjoining church yard, where his memorial monument reminds the passer-by of the vene-

---

* It must also be remembered in considering this statement, that during his ministry, several new churches had been formed, in the bounds, or in the outskirts of his congregation, which frequently decreased the number of his families and church members. Middlebush, Raritan 2nd, Greggstone, Bound Brook, and Raritan 3rd, (Dutch,) were thus formed, besides some Methodist Churches.

rable " *Minister of God*," of more than half a century's service.

The congregation had for some time before his death thought of calling a colleague, but did not do so till the spring of 1850, when Rev. John DeWitt was invited to such position. His call was approved on June 25th, and the time of his installation fixed for August 20th. But five days before the time fixed for the installation, Mr. Zabriskie died.

The following year the Consistory provided the present parsonage property, consisting of a little more than three acres of land, which they bought of John Van Doren, for $755.* They immediately built the pleasant and substantial house, which now adorns the plot, using for this purpose certain legacies which had been left by members, for the support of the Gospel at Millstone. They considered that this was putting those legacies in a permanent shape.†

During Dr. DeWitt's ministry here, the church building having reached more than a quarter of a century of age, was thoroughly repaired, and the pews and pulpit modified to their present neat and beautiful appearance, and the walls

* Beginning at south-west corner of Dr. Wm. McKissack's land, in the road, thence running south 87¼° east, 6 ch. 23 links, north 2° west, 1 ch. 38 links, south 88° east, 4 ch. 52 links, to west bank of the Millstone, thence up said river south 9¼° east, 1 ch. 78 links, south 79¾° west, 3 ch. 51 links, south 19½° east, 1 ch. 95 links, north 70¼° west, 7 ch. 96 links, to middle of the road, down which, north 4¾° west, 2 ch. 79 links, to place of beginning, containing 3 2-100 acres.

† Hendrick Wilson, who died about 1800, left about $1,000, (it is said,) to the Consistory; and Rynier Smock, a few years later, left $375, and Peter Voorhees $500, though this last did not become available till a number of years after his death. (*Search by Ferd. H. Wilson, Esq.*) Possibly there were others, which have not come to the writer's knowledge. These with other moneys which had accumulated, amounted in 1850 to more than $4,000.

frescoed. He received, during his ministry here, two hundred and one on profession of their faith, and seventy-nine by certificate, in all two hundred and eighty, almost the same number as he found to be communicants, at his settlement.* Dr. DeWitt's last report made the church to contain two hundred and ninety-nine members in full communion. His connection with this church ceased on Sept. 1st, 1863, he having accepted the Professorship of Oriental languages and Biblical Exegesis, in our Theological Seminary at New Brunswick, to which he had been elected by General Synod the preceding June. But a short vacancy ensued. Rev. Chs. Stitt was first called, but declined, and your present servant for Jesus' sake was installed, Dec. 29th of the same year. Twenty-eight by profession, and thirty-seven by certificate, in all sixty-five, have been received into the communion of this church during your present relations. Our last report to Classis made three hundred and eleven communicants.

As we look back over our church's history, it is certainly a remarkable fact, and worthy of being mentioned, that five of the seven preceding pastors of this church, were called sooner or later to a professorship in our Theological Seminary, viz., Froeligh, Van Harlingen, Cannon, Schureman, and DeWitt. The other two—Messrs. Foering and Zabriskie—died in the exercise of their pastoral office here.† It is doubtful whether many other churches can show a similar record.

There have been received in this church during the century, eight hundred and eighteen persons on profession, and

* The church of East Millstone, organized in 1855, took a number of families and sixteen members, besides the Methodists, some. Branchville, also organized in 1855, probably affected the church of Millstone to some extent.

† See Appendix, Note 6, for Pastors and Officers.

three hundred and twenty-nine by certificates from other churches, in all, eleven hundred and forty-seven. But making allowance for the loss of the records of four years, and possibly of the accidental omission of some names, (which we have good reason to suppose to have been the case,) the actual number of communicants in this church has been about twelve hundred,* of which a little more than two-thirds were received by profession of faith. Not that this, indeed, is the actual amount of good done by this church, during all this time. There have been undoubtedly other unnumbered, silent influences, whose results can never be gathered up in figures and in history. Many a truth here dropped from the pulpit or from the faithful Christian, may have lain buried in the recesses of the heart for years, and at last, and in other places, blossomed and have borne fruit unto eternal life, perhaps when its possessor stood on the very borders of the grave. Other influences likewise have gone forth, as far as we have helped to send the Gospel through other agencies, to our own western and to foreign lands, and to sustain the institutions of education and religion in their various forms. In faith, something has thus been accomplished, though we cannot point out the definite, specific fruits, for our benevolence was thrown in a common treasury with that of the church in general. The records on high will show what we have done in these respects, how little or how much. But as far as we can ascertain by our records, eight hundred and eighteen in these courts, have been brought to the acknowledgment of Jesus Christ as their only and all sufficient Savior. This, in our own homes, has visibly been our century's work,—a fraction more than eight a year. And while in many respects it may be an unfair comparison, to

* See Appendix—Note 7.

average the *ostensible* success of the respective pastors, yet when done in a proper spirit, and properly understood, it is certainly interesting and perhaps may not be unprofitable for reflection. During the vacancy before the first pastor, of eight years, ten were received on profession, or at the rate of one and a quarter a year; and the number received on profession under the respective pastors, per year on an average, is as follows:—Under Foering, four; under Froeligh, seven; under Van Harlingen, four; under Cannon, three and three-quarters; under Schureman, eight and a half; under Zabriskie, ten and three-quarters; under DeWitt, sixteen and three-quarters; and since his departure, the additions, by profession, have averaged a little more than eleven a year. We should resolve and pray that these numbers, with each advancing decade, may be vastly increased. What a glorious thing, if on an average, for successive terms of years, each week could witness at least one brought to Christ. Let us set this standard, high as it now appears, before us, until having reached it, we may displace it for something better. Let us remember that each church represents the kingdom of heaven on earth, and that it should be our unceasing effort, by means direct and indirect, in public and in private, at home and abroad, to advance the interests of that kingdom. Let us pray that we may begin this century with a new and higher, and advance with an ever-increasing, life. Let us henceforth seek to have *definite* results to show in the foreign field as well as at home. Yea, let each succeeding year, till the Saviour's promise of the universal triumph of his kingdom, be completely realized, witness an ever accelerating progress in piety and philanthropy, which two are the fulfilling of the Law,—the realization, and the exhibition of the restored image of a perfect and divine LOVE.

APPENDIX.

NOTE 1.

The Subscription List for the Building of the First Church, Dec. 6th, 1766.

	£	s.	d.		£	s.	d.
Peter Schenck	38	0	0	Derrick Kroesen	6	0	0
Josiys Cornel	12	0	0	Rocloff Van Aersdalen	7	0	0
Ab. VanBueren	10	0	0	Peter Stryker, Jr	1	15	0
Johannes Hogelandt	10	0	0	Wm. Corteljon	6	0	0
Cor. Van Lewe	14	0	0	Rullef Terheune	6	0	0
Rem Ditmars	14	0	0	Jacobus Garretson	7	0	0
Rem Gerritsen	10	0	0	Rynie VanHengelen	7	0	0
Gerret Terheune	15	0	0	Ouke Rynierse	3	10	0
John Smock	5	0	0	Hendk. VanderVeer	5	0	0
Jan Vander Veer	14	0	0	Stephen Terheune	8	0	0
Hendk. Wilson	14	0	0	Johannes ———	4	10	0
Peter Stryker	12	0	0	Joseph VanderVeer	8	0	0
Chathrine Stryker	3	10	0	Laurence Vancleef	3	1	6
Cornelius Lott	10	10	0	Tise Smock	3	10	0
John Stryker	5	0	0	Wm. George Prall	4	0	0
John VanDoren	14	0	0	Jacobus Stryker	4	0	0
Jurias VanCleef	7	0	6	Yacobus Messelar	1	8	0
Hendk. Probasco	12	0	0	Wm. Spader	3	10	0
Grietie Cornell	3	0	0	Jacob Wyckof	3	10	0
John Ditmars	2	0	0	Johannes Van Zandt	0	8	0
Peter Wyckoff	7	0	0	Ab. Brokaw	2	0	0
Bergen Covert, Jr	3	10	0	Tobias VanNorden	1	10	0
Daniel Covert	4	0	0	Folkerd Buse	2	0	0
Hend. Schenck	25	0	0	Jacob Buse, Jr	3	10	0
John Brokaw	12	0	0	Denice Van Lewe	3	10	0
Cor. Cornell	1	15	0	Barnardus Gerretsen	4	10	5
John Probasco	8	0	0	Peter Wickoff, Sr	1	8	5
Bergon Huff	3	10	0	Jan Kroesen	4	0	0
Ab. Messeler	1	15	0	Corn. Wyckof	2	10	5
John Blaw	1	8	0	Johs. Levdt	3	10	0
Altie Dorlant	1	10	0	Wm. Williamson	1	1	0

	£	s.	d.		£	s.	d.
Wm. Williamson, Jr	0	14	0	Wm. Vliet	1	0	0
Phillip Fulkerson	2	10	0	Peter Sedam	0	15	0
- Peter VanPelt	1	3	4	Wilhelmus Stoothof	1	5	0
Jocham Quick	2	10	0	Nicholas Johnson	1	3	4
Ouke VanHengelen	1	10	0	Hendk. Cortelyou	1	3	4
Corn. Stotehoff	4	0	0	Jaques Cortelyou	1	0	0
Simon Hegeman	1	10	0	Jaques Stoothof	1	0	0
Benj. Hegeman	2	0	0	Peter Staats	4	0	0

NOTE 2.

March 6, 1777.

We, the subscribers, promise to pay, or cause to be paid, to the Consistory of the Church of Hillsborough, the sums annexed to each of our names, for the use of the last payment of the Parsonage.

	£	s.	d.		£	s.	d.
Peter Schenck	18	0	0	Ab. VanDoren	2	5	0
Gerret Terheune	10	0	0	Peter Blaw	1	10	0
Ernestus Van Harlingen	15	0	0	John Blaw	1	15	0 -
John J. Schenck	8	5	0	Isaac Huff	1	2	6
Hendrick Wilson	11	5	0	Cyrenius Thompson	3	0	3
Corn. Cornell	11	5	0	Peter Stryker, son of Peter	10	0	0
— Hendrick Probasco	10	0	0	Benj. Brokaw	3	15	0
Ab. Van Beuren, M.D	10	1	0	Peter Stryker, L. Island	15	0	0
John Van Doren	15	0	0	Isaac Van Nuys	6	0	0
Fulkert Buys	6	7	6	Myndert Willson	3	0	0
Peter Ditmars	15	0	0	Johannes VanZandt	3	0	0
Laurance Vander Veer	17	2	6	John Christopher	1	10	0
Peter Staats	11	5	0	John Stryker	10	5	9
Jacob Boyce	3	5	0	John Nowlen	1	10	0
Jacobus Gerretson	11	5	0	Coonraat Van Wagenner	1	2	6
Ab. Ditmarse	9	0	0	Brogone Brokaw	1	10	0
Isaac Van Cleef	1	2	6	Christn. VanArsdalen Taylor	1	2	8
Johanes Hoogdland	11	5	0	Ann Van Lewe, widow	10	0	0
J. Van Cleef	6	0	0	Benj. Arrosmith	0	15	0
Wm. Willson	1	14	6	John Smock	1	10	1
John Bennett	11	5	0	Abm. Duryea	11	5	0
Nicholas Cowenhoven	9	10	0	Joseph Cornell	3	0	0
Sam. Davis	0	15	0	Peter Wyckoff	11	5	0
Cornelius Lott	15	0	0	Peter Schenck, Jr	11	5	0
Laurence Van Cleef	15	0	0	Albert Cornell	9	0	0
Philip Fulkerson	1	10	0	Covert Voorheese	00	15	0
John Scheurman	2	5	0	Garret Terheune, Jr	11	5	0
— John Probasco	3	15	0	Rem Gerritson	11	5	0

	£	s.	d.		£	s.	d.
Michael VanderVeer.........	7	10	2	Stephen Terheune............	3	0	0
Thomas VanDike.............	3	4	6	John Ditmarse...............	3	0	0
John VanderVeer............11		5	0	John Staats, Jr...............	3	0	0
Peter Stryker................	1	10	0	Elsye Ryneerson..............	0	10	0
Garret Van Cleef.............	1	10	0	Jacobus VanNuys, son of John	0	10	0
Nic. Van Brandt.............	3	15	0	Corn. VanNuys, " "	0	15	0
Wm. Cortelyou..............	7	10	0	Garret R. Garretson..........11		5	0
Teunis Covert................	3	0	0	Lucas Voorheese............	2	0	0

NOTE 3.

AFTER the war, they found themselves **unable to repair the church, owing to** the ravages **of the** raiding parties, &c., **and therefore the Consistory issued the** following appeal for help :—

Whereas the Dutch Reformed Congregation of New Millstone, in the County of Somerset, and State of New Jersey, has been **much distressed by the late destruc**tive **war,** the inhabitants plundered of their property, their church in part destroyed, and rendered useless; and whereas said congregation is by such sufferings rendered in a manner incapable of repairing their church :—We, the subscribers, Elders and Deacons of said congregation, find ourselves under the *disagreeable necessity* of applying for assistance to the brethren of our profession, and especially to those whom a kind Providence has protected against similar distress; who from pure motives of sympathy, we trust, will be induced to charity and benevolence. And in order to promote this, our purpose, we have appointed and authorized our Pastor, the Rev. Solomon Froeligh, Capt. **Cor. Lott,** and **Peter Ditmarse,** to present this our application to such of our brethren, as they from personal acquaintance, or recommendation, may deem persons of a benevolent disposition, and to assure them **from us,** that their donations will be received with gratitude, **and their names perpetuated** on the records **of our church, as examples of gener**osity by their   Humble servants.

	Elders.	*Deacons.*
Signed.	AB. VAN BEUREN,	AB. DITMARSE,
	CORNELIUS CORNELL,	PETER WYKOFF,
	HEND. PROBASCO,	GARRIT R. GARRETSON,
	JOHN STRYKER,	FULKERT BUYS.

	£	s.	d.		£	s.	d.
Jeremiah Van Derbilt...........1		17	4	Mathias Vandyk................1		17	4
John Ryerson..................1		17	4	Nicalaus Vandyk...............1		17	4
Martin Skenk..................1		17	4	John Johnson..................1		17	4
Anne Johnson.................1		17	4	Johannes De Bevois............1		12	0
Abraham Remsen..............1		17	4	John R. Couwenhoven..........1		17	4
Jacob Byerson.................1		17	4	John Cowenhoven..............1		17	4
Rem A. Remsen................1		17	4	Lamberth Suydam..............1		17	4

	£	s.	d.		£	s.	d.
Leffert Leffertse	1	17	4	Hend. Vanderveer	1	4	0
Barent Leffertse	1	17	4	Jas. J. VanBuren	0	16	0
Jacobus Lott and } Widow Johnson }	0	10	0	Jer. Vanderbilt	1	4	0
				Peter Lafferts	1	12	0
Barent Johnson	0	8	0	Seytie Hegeman	0	16	0
Johannes Stoothoff	0	8		Leffert Martinse	0	16	0
Peter Vanderbilt	0	8	0	Peter Cornell	0	16	0
Jeromus Lott	1	4	0	Philippus Nagle	1	4	0
Petrus Lott	1	17	4	Joris Martise	1	12	0
Jeremiah Vanderbilt	0	16	4	John Vanderbilt	1	17	4
Abraham Voorhees	1	4	0	Dr. Hend. VanBuren	0	12	0
Fulkert Sprough	0	16	0	John Hegeman	0	8	0
Johannes Ditmarse	2	13	4	Leffert Leffertse	0	8	0
Peter Cowehoven	0	16	0	Jacob Leffertse	1	8	0
Johannes Remsen	1	4	0	John Beuren	0	8	0
Derick Remsen	0	12	0	Garret Stryker	1	4	0
John Williamson	0	8	0	Peter Antonides	1	17	4
John Vanderveer	0	18	8	Henry Staats	0	16	0
Nicolaus Wykoff	1	4	0	Hendk. Suydam	0	16	0
Teunis Skenk	1	12	0	Jacob Suydam	0	16	0
Gabriel Duryee	0	16	0	Johannes E. Lott	1	17	4
Johannes Titus	0	12	0	Hendk. Suydam	0	16	0
Ab. Laquier	1	17	6	John Striker	0	16	0
Corn. Vanderveer	1	17	4	Thomas Elseworth	0	16	0
John Ditmarse	1	17	4	Elias Hubbard	0	16	0
Arjaantje Voorhees, widow	1	4	0	Isaac Stover	0	8	0
Jacobus Vanderveer	1	17	4	Garrit Wykoff	0	10	0
Rem Hegeman	0	18	8				
				£85	**0**	**0**	

NOTE 4.

THE valleys of the Raritan and its tributaries, are now comparatively well supplied with churches. While in the year 1700, there was only one of the Dutch name, there are now more than thirty on the same territory, not to speak of the many of other denominations. Besides the Dutch churches referred to in this discourse, the following have been organized in later years, viz. :—

WHITEHOUSE, (1793,) to which successively have ministered Revs. John Duryee, (1799-1801,) Cor. T. Demarest, (1808-13,) Jac. I. Schultz, (1816-34,) Peter S. Williamson, (1835-39,) Jas. Otterson, (1840-45,) Goyn Talmage, (1845-51,) Lawrence Comfort, (1852-54,) Aaron Lloyd, (1855-56,) Smith Sturges, (1857-63,) and Evert Van Slyke, since 1864 :—

LEBANON, (1813,) Revs. Jac. I. Schultz, (1816-34,) Chs. P. Wack, (1835-40,) Robt. VanAmburgh, (1840-48,) John Steele, (1848-53,) and Robt. VanAmburgh again, since 1853 :—

SPOTTSWOOD, (1821,) Revs. John McClure, (1822–25,) Henry L. Rice, (1825–34,) John C. Van Liew, (1834–42,) Wm. R. S. Betts, (1842–45,) William Knight, (1846–47,) John H. Manning, (1847–54,) and A. Vandewater, since 1855 :—

NORTH BRANCH, (1825,) Revs. George H. Fisher, (1826–30,) Ab. D. Wilson, (1831–38,) Jas. K. Campbell, (1839–54,) and Philip W. Doolittle, since 1856 :—

BLAWENBURGH, (1832,) Revs. Henry Heermance, (1832–35,) Jas. R. Talmage, (1836–48,) Theodore B. Romeyn, (1849–65,) and C. W. Fritts, since 1865 :—

MIDDLEBUSH, (1834,) Revs. Jac. I. Schultz, (1834–38,) John A. VanDoren, (1838–66,) and Geo. W. Swayne, the present pastor :—

CLOVER HILL, (1834,) Revs. Garret C. Schenck, (1835–36,) William Demarest, (1837–39,) after this, this church became Presbyterian, but subsequently returned to the Dutch denomination, and Rev. W. B. Voorhees has labored there since 1864 :—

RARITAN 2ND, (1834,) Revs. Chs. Whitehead, (1835–39,) Talbot W. Chambers, (1840–49,) Elijah R. Craven, (1850–54,) and John F. Mesick, since 1855 :—

NEW BRUNSWICK 2ND, (1842,) Revs. David D. Demarest, (1843–52,) Samuel M. Woodbridge, (1852–57,) Hugh M. Wilson, (1858–62,) and John W. Schenck, (1863–66,) and at present without a pastor :—

GRIGGSTOWN, (1842,) Revs. Jer. S. Lord, (1843–49,) John A. Todd, (1849–55,) Edward P. Livingston, (1855–58,) and Stephen T. Searle, since 1859 :—

BOUND BROOK, (1846,) Revs. Geo. J. Van Nest, (1848–53,) Wm. Demarest, (1854–57,) Henry V. Voorhees, (1858–62,) and Benj. F. Romaine, since 1862 :—

RARITAN 3RD, (1848,) Revs. Peter Stryker, (1848–51,) Jas. A. H. Cornell, (1852–56,) and Jas. Le Fevre, since 1857 :—

PEAPACK, (1848,) Revs. Wm. A. Anderson, (1849–56,) and Henry P. Thompson, since 1857 :—

NEW BRUNSWICK 3RD, *German*, (1851,) Rev. Francis M. Serenbetts, (1851–54,) Franz M. Schneeweiss, (1855–58,) Julius Hones, *stated supply*, (1858–60,) Carl Meyer, *stated supply*, (1863–64,) and T. Cludius, since 1865 :—

BRANCHVILLE, (1850,) Revs. Henry Dater, (1851–53,) and Wm. Pitcner, since 1854 :—

EAST MILLSTONE, (1855,) Revs. Giles Vandewall, (1856–58,) David Cole, (1858–63,) Martin L. Berger, (1863–66,) and Wm. H. Phraner, the present pastor :—

WARREN, *German*, (1856,) Revs. John H. Oerter, (1856–58,) Jacob F. Neef, *stated supply*, (1858–60, *pastor* 1860–64,) and Wm. Wolf, since 1865 :—

ROCKY HILL, (1857,) Revs. Martin L. Schenck, (1857–64,) and O. Gesner, since 1865 :—

METUCHEN, (1857,) Rev. J. B. Thompson, since 1859 :—

PLAINFIELD, *German*, (1858,) Revs. Jacob F. Neef, *stated supply*, (1858–60, *pastor*, 1860–64,) and Wm. Wolf, since 1865 :—

CENTRAL PLAINFIELD, (1863,) Rev. John Simonson, since 1863 :—

POTTERSVILLE, (1865,) without pastor :—

HIGH BRIDGE, (1865,) without pastor :—

In reference to the older churches, (to take up the line in brief, where it was dropped in the discourse,)—Rev. John S. Vredenburgh having labored at RARITAN for twenty-two years, died in 1821, and his successors are Revs. Richard D. Van Kleek, (1826–31,) and Abraham Messler, since 1832 :—

Rev. Jas. Romeyn, succeeded Dr. Cannon at Six Mile Run, (1828–33,) and Rev. Jacob C. Sears, since 1833 :—

Rev. Jesse Fonda succeeded Dr. John Schureman at New Brunswick, (1814–17,) and his successors are Revs. John Ludlow, (1817–19,) Isaac M. Ferris, (1821–24,) Jas. B. Hardenbergh, (1825–29,) Jacob J. Janeway, (1830–31,) Sam. B. How, who labored in this field for a generation, (1832–61,) and Rich. H. Steele, since 1863 :—

Rev. John Van Liew succeeded to the pastorate of the church of Readington in 1828, made vacant by the death of Dr. Studdiford in 1826 :—

Rev. Peter Labagh was called in 1809, to succeed Rev. Henry Polhemus at Harlingen and Neshanic, and as colleague of Rev. Wm. R. Smith, who continued to serve these congregations till 1817, when with increasing infirmities, (though only sixty-four years of age,) he resigned, and died in 1820. Mr. Labagh served the two churches till 1821, when he limited his services to Harlingen alone, till 1844, when he resigned, and Rev. John Gardner succeeded him, in the same year, and is the present pastor; while Rev. Gabriel Ludlow succeeded Mr. Labagh at Neshanic, in 1821, and still continues to serve that church :—

After the single year of service of Rev. Theodore F. Romeyn, at Bedminster, (1785–86,) Rev. Mr. Studdiford, of Readington, united this church with his other charge, (1787–1800,) and Rev. John Duryee succeeded him, (1800–1,) and subsequently have ministered there, Revs. John Schureman, (1801–7,) Charles Hardenbergh, (1808–20,) I. M. Fisher, (1821–39,) Geo. Schenck, (1840–52,) William Brush,(1852–65,) and Charles H.Poole, since 1865 :—Thus the valleys of the Raritan and its tributaries, in early times so poorly supplied with Gospel privileges, have been even in reference to our single denomination, most signally blessed of Providence, in the large multiplication of churches and of pastors.   There are now no less than thirty-one churches and forty-one ministers on the territory, whose history we have been considering, and three-fourths of these ministers are settled pastors.   If the material were at hand to show the numbers and conditions of the churches of other denominations, on the same ground, the benevolence of Providence toward this region would appear indeed most wonderful.   It has often been called " The Garden of the Church."   God has here richly poured out His Spirit, time and again.   All the records of the older congregations, and of many of the younger, show unwonted numbers of accessions to the church.   The bold, true, evangelical, untrammelled spirit of faith, of the first pastors, and of the second and third generations, in these valleys, and their earnest, importunate prayers, seem to have commanded God's blessing upon their children, and their children's children.   But let us not fail to remember that the greatness of these former blessings constitutes now a source of danger.   All history confirms this.   It must be our own earnest, diligent, ardent piety, conformed to the new and wonderful developments of Providence, which alone can retain and increase these heavenly experiences of the past.   Let us prove ourselves worthy of our birthright, by our fidelity to the cause of God and man.   Where much is given, much will be required.

NOTE 5.

List of Members for the year 1801.

* Peter Wykoff,
Jochamyntic Vechter
Wm. Cortelyou
Eve Terhune
Jacob Garretson
Magdalene Ditmars
Isaac Van Nuys
Nelly Quick
Rynier Smock
T. Van Arsdaalen
Geertic Rynierson
Michael Vander Veer
Peter Stryker
Maria Van Nortwick
Thomas Drue
Phebe Dumont
Peter Voorhees
Cath. Skilman
Peter Staats
Susannah Van Middleswort
John Zutphen
Gerardus Voorhees
Mary Quick
Wm. Wykoff
Elizabeth ———
Cath. Van Matic, w. of H. Disbury
Barent Cornell
Cath. Stathoff
John Staats, Sr.
Charity Quick
John Staats, Jr.
Mary Vechter
Susannah Staats
Martin Schenck
Marg. Schureman

Altye Wykoff w. of Josiah Schenck
Ab. Van Bueren
Elizabeth Krusen
Jacobus Garretson, Jr.
Martha Vechter
Judith, widow of Sam. Williams.
Isaac Lott
Phamatic Ditmars
Gerret Gerritson
John Nevius
Phamatie Staats
Dr. Peter Stryker
Helena Schenck
Jane Rice
Maria, widow of John Hardenberg
Williampje, widow of Corn. Cornell
Williampje, wid. of Gerret Schureman
John Van Doren, Jr.
Nelly Lott
John Bainbridge
Anantje Dumont
Ernestus VanHarlingen
Maria Othout
Catharine Blauw
Maty Ditmars, w. of Jacob VanDoren
Maria, widow of Peter Ditmars
Altje VanDoren, w. of Teunis Hoagland
Elizabeth, wife of Fred. Probasco
Matie Lott, w. of John VanDoren, Jr.
Cyrenius Thompson
Tone, slave of Rynier Smock
Thomas, slave of P. Wykoff
Jack, slave of P. Ditmars
Nelly, slave of T. VanDoren
Peg, slave of Wm. Cortelyou.

A Register of the Members of the Church at Millstone in full communion, in 1805 *and* 1806.

1. Peter VanDoren, by certif.from New Shannick, Nov. 11, 1784.
2. Elizabeth Kennedy, w. of Frederick Probasco, 1783.
3. Rynier Smock,
4. Areantje Van Arsdalen, Nov. 15, 1769.
5. Garrit K. Garritson, Nov. 24, 1780.
6. Williampje Wykoff, Nov. 24, 1780.

* These braces indicate husband and wife.

7. Ariantje Dumond, w. of John Bainbridge, Dec. 6, 1781.
8. Cyrenius Thompson, Dec. 6, 1781.
9. John VanDoren, Jr.,   "   "
10. Catrina Summers, w. of Sam. Davis,
    Dec. 6, 1781.
11. { Peter Wykoff,   Oct. 24, 1782.
12. { Jacamyntja Vechta,   "   "
13. { William Cortelyou,
14. { Eva Terhune,   "   "
15. **Maria Schenck, w. of A. Mercer,**
    Oct. 24, 1782.
16. Rebecca Sikkelsa, w. of C. Thomp-
    son, Oct. 24, 1782.
17. John Van Harlingen, Oct. 24, 1782.
18. { Jacobus Garritson,   1785–1805.
19. { Lena Ditmars,
20. { Barent Cornell,
21. { Catherine Stothoff,
22. Ernestus Van Harlingen,
23. { Abraham Van Beuren,
24. { Elizabeth Kruzen,
25. { Peter Stryker,
26. { Maria Nortwick,
27. { Peter Staats,
28. { Susannah Middleswort,
29. Williampje Ditmars, widow
    of Corn. Cornell,
30. John Bainbridge,

31. Frederick Probasco, 1785–1805.
32. { Joseph Cornell,
33. { Tana Van Nuys,
34. { Garrit Wykoff,
35. { Rachel Croesen,
36. { Martin Schenck,
37. { Margaret Schureman,
38. { John Nevius,
39. { Phamatja Staats,
40. Peter T Stryker,
41. { Peter Voorhees,
42. { Cath. Skillman,
43. John Zutphen,
44. { Gerardus Voorhees,
45. { Maria Quick,
46. Eleanor Lott, w. of John Van
    Doren, Jr.,
47. Michael VanderVeer,
48. Stephen Garritson,
49. Maria Perrine, w. of G. K.
    Garritson,
50. Eusannah Staats,
51. Geertje Rynierson,
52. Ann Yard, widow of Fred.
    Frelinghuysen,
53. Rem Garritson,
54. Jacobus Van Nuys,
55. Lucy Mercer, wid. of John
    Frelinghuysen.

NOTE 6.

Pastors.

1720....**THEODORE J.** FRELINGHUYSEN....1747.
Over the churches of Raritan, Three Mile Run, New Brunswick, Six Mile Run,
North Branch, (now Readington,) and Millstone, (now Harlingen,) *after* 1729.

1748....JOHN LEYDT....1783.
Over the churches of New Brunswick and Six Mile Run.

1750....JOHN FRELINGHUYSEN....1754.
Over the churches of Raritan, Readington, and Millstone, (now Harlingen).

1758....JACOB R. HARDENBERGH....1781.
Over the churches of Raritan, Readington, Bedminster, Millstone, (now Harlingen,)
and Nechanic. In 1761 he visited Holland, and in 1763 returned, and took
charge of the first three of these churches again till 1781.

1762....John M. Van Harlingen....1795.
Over the churches of Nechanic and Millstone, (now Harlingen).

The original Dutch inhabitants of Millstone Valley, were under the ministries of these several pastors, before the organization of the church at New Millstone, (now called the church of Hillsborough,) in **1766.**

Pastors of the Church of New Millstone, or Hillsborough.

1767.   Arrangements were made with Messrs. Leydt, Hardenbergh and Van Harlingen, to supply the pulpit once a month in turns.   1774.

1774....Christian Frederick Foering....1779.

1780....Solomon Froeligh....1786.
. In connection with Nechanic.

1787....John M. Van Harlingen....1795.
[Nephew of John M. Van Harlingen at Millstone, (now Harlingen,)]
In connection with Six Mile Run.

1797....James Spencer Cannon....1807.
In connection with Six Mile Run.

1807....John Schureman....1809.

1811....John Lansing Zabriskie....1850.

1850....John DeWitt....1863.

Edward Tanjore Corwin.
1863.

Church Officers.

	Elders.	Deacons.
Aug. 1776.	Joseph Cornel,	Johannes Hogelandt,
	Peter Schenck,	Abraham Van Beuren, M.D.,
1770.*	Ernestus Van Harlingen,	Jan Probasco,
Apr., 1775.*	Garret Terhune, Sr.,	Henry Wilson,
Nov., 1775.	Peter Schenck, Esq.,	Cor. Van Lewen,
	Peter Stryker, Sr.,	Cor. Cornell,
Aug., 1778.	Ernestus Van Harlingen,	John Probasco,
	Garret Terhune,	Hendrick Probasco,
June, 1780.	Ab. Van Beuren, M.D.,	John Stryker,
	Peter Stryker,	Jacobus Gerrison,
Aug., 1781.	Garret Terhune,	Peter Ditmarse,
	Ernestus Van Harlingen,	Benj. Broca,
Nov., 1781.	Lucas Nevius,†	
June, 1782.	Cor. Cornell,	Ab. Ditmarse,
	Hendrick Probasco,	Garret R.,Garretse.

*These were added to the original officers to increase the number, at the respective dates, the Consistory now for the first containing eight in 1775.
†In place of Gerret Terhune deceased.

	Elders.	Deacons.
June, 1783.	Ab. Van Beuren, M.D.,	Folkert Buys,
	John Stryker,	Peter Wykhoff.
1784.	Jacobus Garretse	Philip Van Nortwyck,
	Peter Ditmarse,	John VanderVeer.
July, 1785.	Peter VanDoren,	Albert Cornell,
	Benj. Broca,	Tunis Coevert.
Dec., 1785.		John VanDoren.*
Nov., 1787.	Peter Wykoff,†	Garret Terhune,
	Folkert Buys,	Wm. Corteljou.
June, 1788.	Hendrick Probasco,	Adam Smith,
	Ernestus Van Harlingen,	Peter Stryker.
May, 1789.	Ab. Ditmars,	John Stryker,
	Cor. Cornell,	Joseph Cornell.
July, 1790.	Jacobus Garretson,	John VanDoren,
	Teunis Coevert,	Peter Van Lewen.
1791.	Peter Ditmars,	Michael VanderVeer,
	Peter Stryker,	John VanderVeer.
1792.	Folkert Buys,	Isaac Van Nuys,
	Peter Wyckoff,	Peter Nevius.
May, 1793.	Cor. Cornell,	Cyrenius Thompson,
	Jacobus Garretson,	Barent Cornell.
Aug., 1794.	Ab. Ditmars,	John VanDoren,
	Peter Stryker,	Garret R. Garretson.
1795.	Peter Wyckoff,	John VanderVeer,
	Ab. Van Beuren, M.D.,	Joseph Cornell.
Sep., 1797.	Gerrit Terhune,‡	Isaac Van Nuys,
	Rynier Smock,	John Nevius.
1798.	Jacobus Garretson,	Peter Staats,
	Wm. Korteljou	Wm. Wykoff.
	John VanDoren, Jr.,§	
Nov. 1799.	Peter Stryker,	Jacobus Garretson,
	John VanDoren, Jr.,	Peter Stryker, M.D.
Oct., 1800.	Peter Wykoff,	Martin Schenck,
	John Nevius,	Gerardus Voorhees.
1801.	Rynier Smock,	John Bainbridge,
	John Staats, Sr.,	Thomas Drue.
Oct., 1802.	Ab. Van Beuren, M.D.,	Peter Voorhees,
	Barent Cornell,	Isaac Lott.
Nov. 1803.	Peter Stryker,	John Staats,
	Peter VanDoren,	Garret Wyckoff.
1804.	Isaac Van Nuys,	Fred. Probasco.
	Wm. Wykoff,	John Zutphen.
Oct., 1805.	Jacobus Garretson,	Joseph Cornell,

*In place of Philip Van Nortwyck. †Election omitted in 1786.
‡No election in 1796. § In place of Gerret Terhune, deceased.

Elders.	*Deacons.*
	Peter Staats,	Myndert Wilson.
Nov., 1806.	Peter Wykoff,	Gerardus Voorhees,
	Garret R. Garretson,	Martin Schenck.
Oct., 1807.	John Bainbridge,	Ab. Whiteneck,
	John Van Doren, Jr.,	Stephen Garretson,
		Peter Voorhees.*
May, 1809.	Rynier Smock,	Hendrick Wilson,
	Peter J. Stryker, M.D.,	Garret Wyckoff.
1810.	Ab. Van Beuren, M.D.,	Farrington Barcaloo.
	Jacobus Garretson,	Urias Van Cleef.
1811.	Peter Stryker,	Isaac Lott,
	Barent Cornell,	John Staats.
1812.	Martin Schenck, Esq.,	Ab. Staats,
	Peter Voorhees,	Peter Williamson.
1813.	John Bainbridge,	Isaac Lott,
	Wm. Wycoff,	Rem Garritson.
1814.	John Van Doren,	Peter Gerretson,
	Gerrit Wycoff,	Joshia Schenck.
1815.	Gerrit Gerritsen,	John D. Ditmars,
	Henry Wilson, .	Urias Van Cleef.
1816.	Peter Stryker,	Abraham D. Baird,
	Barent Cornell,	John I. Staats.
1817.	Ruliff Terhune,	John Broach,
	Martin Schenck,	Aaron Prawl.
1818.	Rem Gerritson,	Peter Williamson,
	John VanDoren,	John Stryker.
1819.	Ab. I. Staats,	Edward Van Harlingen,
	Myndard Wilson,	Ab. Beekman.
1820.	Gerritt Wycoff,	Nicholas Bainbridge,
	Farrington Barcaloo,	Corn. Van Nuys.
1821.	John Staats,	Isaac VanCleef,
	John Bainbridge,	Mile Root.
1822.	Peter Gerritson,	John M. Wycoff,
	Urias Van Cleef,	Henry Staats.
1823.	Stephen Gerritson,	Joseph Christopher,
	Roeliff Terhune,	John Wilson.
1824.	Rem Gerritson,	Isaac Van Nuys,
	Edward Van Harlingen,	Cornelius Covenhoven.
1825.	Ab. Staats,	Gerrit Gerritson,
	John Van Doren,	John Van Zandt.
1826.	John Sutphen,	John Wycoff,
	Ab. Beekman,	Abm. Davis.
1827.	John D. Ditmars,	Henry Stryker,
	Farrington Barcaloo,	John VanderVeer.

*In place of S. Garretson, moved away.

	Elders.	Deacons.
1828.	John Staats, Peter Gerritson,	Jacob Van Cleef, Corn. VanNuys.
1829.	Roeliff Terhune, Stephen Gerritson,	Josiah Schenck, Isaac V. C. Stryker.
1830.	Peter Williamson, Isaac Lott,	Douw Ditmars, Wm. Blackwell.
1831.	Isaac Van Cleef, Ab. Staats, Stephen Gerritson.*	Jacob Schenck, Henry Wilson.
1832.	Cornelius Covenhoven, Garret Wycoff,	Jas. G. Quick, Christopher Hoagland.
1833.	Isaac Van Nuys, Urias Van Cleef,	Peter I. Smith, Peter L. Sebring.
1834.	John Wilson, John V. M. Wyckoff,	Sam. Wyckoff, Rynier Staats.
October.	Peter Gerritson,	Ab. A. Quick.
1835.	John Ditmars, Joseph Christopher,	Peter Van Nest, Ernest Schenck.
1836.	Ab. Beekman, John Vanderveer,	Cor. Staats, John Sutphen.
1837.	Ab. Staats, John Van Zandt,	Peter Nevius, John J. Stryker.
1838.	Jacob S. Van Cleef, Cornelius Van Nuys,	Henry C. Stryker, John P. Staats, John J. Ditmars.†
1839.	John M. Wyckoff, Jacob Schenck,	John J. Staats, Isaac Cornell.
1840.	Henry P. Staats, Henry H. Wilson,	John W. Smock, Ralph T. Sutphen.
1841.	Rynier Staats, Ab. Quick,	Evert Bergen, Peter Wyckoff.‡
1842.	Christopher Hoagland‡ Isaac Van Nuys,	John A. Smith, Luke S. Vanderveer, John Quick.
1843.	Henry Powelson, Henry P. Stryker,	Wm. French, John Quick.
1844.	Stephen Garretson, Peter Williamson,	Peter N. Beekman, Benj. Smith.
1845.	John J. Ditmars, Isaac V. C. Stryker,	John G. Voorhees, Peter P. Staats.
1846.	Peter J. Nevius, Cor. Van Nuys,	' Alfred French, John Van Doren.
1847.	John I. Staats,	Jas. L. Voorhees,

*In place of Isaac Lott, deceased. †For one year in place of John J. Stryker.
‡Resigned to unite with new church at Griggstown.

Elders.	*Deacons.*
John D. Ditmarse,	Joachim Quick.
1848. Samuel Wyckoff,	J. V. D. Hoagland,
John Wilson,	Joseph ——
1849. Isaac Van Nuys,	John J. Ditmars,*
John P. Staats.	Cor. J. Hulick.
1850. Isaac Van Cleef, Sr.,	Isaac L. Van Cleef,
Ralph T. Sutphen,	Luke S. Vanderveer,
	Wm. French.
1851. Ab. Davis,	Ab. Veghte,
Henry C. Stryker,	Cor. Broach.
1852. John Van Doren,	Cor. J. Hoagland,
Josiah Schenck,	J. L. Oakey.
1853. Peter P. Staats,	Benj. A. Smith,
Jas. L. Voorhees,	John Van Zandt.
1854. Ernestus Schenck.	Jonathan W. Wilson,
Benj. A. Smith,	John V. D. Nevius.
1855. Joachim G. Quick,	John V. A. Merrill,†
Abm. Quick,	Roeliff T. Ditmars,
	Jas. G. Voorhees.
1856. Ab. A. Beekman,	Henry Coleman,
Isaac L. Van Cleef,	Peter S. Williamson.
1857. John M. Wyckoff,	Jacob J. Garretson,
Henry V. Powelson	Peter C. Staats.
1858. Jacob S. Van Cleef,	Wm. Hulce.
John A. Smith,	Peter S. Vanderveer.
1859. Cor. J. Gulick,	Peter S. Ditmars,
Jas. L. Voorhees,	Elijah Rouser.
1860. Peter J. Nevius,	Gershom Bernart,
John V. D. Hoagland,	Wm. M. K. Smith.
1861. John Van Zant,	Wm. Voorhees,
R. T. Sutphen.	Jas. Van Nuys.
1862. John Van Doren,	Peter L. Powelson,.
James J. Garretson,‡	Sanford B. Wakeman.
1863. John P. Staats,	Adrian Merrill,
John J. Staats,	John H. Wilson.
Jas. L. Voorhees.	
1864. Benj. A. Smith,	John Vanderipe,
Peter N. Beekman,	Selah W. Smith.
1865. Henry Van Nuys,‡	John V. Van Nest,
Peter S. Ditmars,	Ab. J. Voorhees.‡
1866. Jas. L. Voorhees,	Cor. H. Broach,
John Smith,	John Staats,
Ralph T. Sutphen,	Fred. T. Smith.

*Resigned on account of removal.

† Resigned.   ‡ Deceased.

NOTE 7.

Members of the Church of Hillsborough.

[c. for Certificate.—b. for baptized.—* for living members.]

Aug., 1766. Joseph Cornell, } Elders.
Peter Schenck, }
Johannes Hogelandt, } Dea-
AbrahamVanBeuren, } cons.
{ Peter Stryker,
{ Catrina Büys,
Hendrick Wilson,
{ Rem Ditmars,
{ Helena Van Lœwe,
{ Stoffel Van Arsdalen,
{ Maghdalen Van Hengelen,
{ Rynier Van Hengelen,
{ Gurtje Van Galen,
Maritje Woortman,
w. of Johan. Hogelandt.
Maritje Prall,
wid. of Aaron Prall.
(*This was the original mem-*
bership (15) *at the organi-*
zation of the church, being
received by certificate from
Raritan, New Brunswick,
Six Mile Run & Harlingen.

Nov., 1769. { Rynier Smock,
{ Arejantje Van Arsdalen,
Bernardus Garretson,
—John Probasco,
Cornelius Lott,
Maria Volkerson,
w. of Peter Schenck,
Ernestus Van Harlingen.

July, 1772. Cornelius Van Leuwen,
Hendrick Probasco,
Cornelius Cornell,
{ Adolph Wever, c.
{ Margaritha Schrom, c.

May, 1775. { Jacobus Gerritson,
{ Helena Ditmars,
Sytie Van Derveer,
wid. of John Van Derveer,
Anne Van Lewen,
w. of Cor. Van Lewen,

Mattie Van Doren,
w. of John Van Doren,
Gertie —— ——,
w. of Jacob Stryker,
Anne —— ——,
w. of Hendrick Probasco,
Henrica —— ——,
w. of Corn. Lott,
Jack,
slave of wid. Ditmars.
Oct., 1775. John Stryker, Sr.,
{ Ab. Ditmars,
{ Cath. Williamson,
{ Rueloff Terhune,
{ Anne Williamson,·
Williampje Ditmars,
w. of Corn. Cornell,
Dina, slave of John Stryker.
April, 1776. Benj. Brokaw,
Elizb. Crusen,
w. of Dr. Van Beuren.
Nov., 1780. Joseph Cornell,
{ Peter Ditmars,
{ Mar. Duryea, or Pomje,
Gerrit R. Gerritson,
Maria Suydam,
w. of Lawrence Van Cleef
Janaatje Laen,
wid. of LawrenceVanCleef,
Williampje Wyk Hoff,
w. of Gerrit Terhune.
Nov., 1781. Lucas Nevius, c.
Dec., 1781. { Lucas Van Voorhees,
{ Johanna Dumond,
Cyrenius Thompson,
{ Teunis Covert,
{ Magdalena Van Hengelen,
{ John Van Dorn,
{ Catalina Van Voorheesen,
Maria Post, w. of J. Bennet,
Nicholas Willemse,
Ariantje Dumond, /

Sarah Auke,
   w. of Benj. Broka,
Cathrina Summers,
   w. of Sam. Davis,
Cornelia Probasco,
   wid. of Peter Montfoort,
Lydia **Cornell,**
   w. of John Stryker,
Catrina Van Wagene,
   w. of Rynier Vegter,
Rachel Vanderbeck,
   w. of Rev. Sol. Froeligh, c.

Oct., 1782. Garret Terhune,
   { Martinus Nevius,
   { Antje Voorheese,
   { Peter Wykoff,
   { Jacamyntje Vegter,
   { Wm. Catteljou,
   { Eva Terhune,
   Maria Schenck,
     w. of Arch. Mercer,
   Matje Cornell,
     w. of Luycas Nevins,
   { **John Vanderveer,**
   { **Janatje Van Pelt,**
   { Folkert Buys,
   { Hendrica Prall,
   Rebekka Sikklese,
     w. of Cyrenius Thompson,
   John Van Harlingen,
   Philip Van Noortwyk,
   { **Albert Cornell, c.**
   { Antje Stryker, c.

June, 1783. Ida Garretse,
     wid. of Uriah Van **Cleef,**
   Annaatje Coevert,
     wid. of Jas. Wright,
   Elizabeth Kennedy,
     w. of Jas. Cornell.

Nov., 1784. Margreta Bennet,
     w. of Peter Ditmarse,
   Peter Van Doren, **c.**

June, 1784. Cytie Dumond,
     w. of Hen. Probasco, c.

May, 1788. Adam Smith, Sr.,
   John Nevius,
   Peter Stryker,

{ John Bennett, Jr.,
{ Jane Van Middleswort,
{ John Stryker,
{ Femmetje Saadam,
{ Peter Van Leuwen,
{ Sytie Wykoff,
Susanna Van Middleswort,
   w. of Peter Staats,
Femmetje Brokaw,
   w. of Benj. Waldron.

June, 1789. Nelly Lott,
   Gertje Lott.

June, 1790. Aaltje Van Doren,
     w. of Tunis Hoagland,
   Sarah Tontein,
     w. of John Hoagland,
   Sarah Titchell,
     wid. of Henry Rodgers,
   Prince
     servt. of Peter Wyckoff, b.
   Judith, and Tyne,
     servts. of Cor. Cornell, b.b.
   Margaret,
     servt. of Wm. Corteljou, b.
   Nelly, ser. of Peter Hoff, b.

July, 1791. Michael Vanderveer,
   Myndert Wilson,
   { Peter Nevius,
   { Maria Terhune,
   Maria Groenendyk,
     w. of Peter Ditmars, c.
   Jannetie Van Arsdalen,
     w. of Myndert Wilson, c.

May, 1792. { Isaac Van Nuys,
      { Nelly Quick,
   { Barent Cornell,
   { Cath. Stoothoff,
   Marg. Schureman,
     w. of Martjn Schenck,
   Sarah,
     servt. of Garret Terhune,
   Sarah,
     serv. of John Wyckoff.

Nov., 1797. { Gerardus Voorhees, c.
      { Mary Quick, c.
   { Rynier Smock, c.
   { T. Van Arsdalen, c.

Ann Hall,
  w. Jacob Probasco, c.
{ Wm. Wyckoff, c.
{ Elizabeth, c.
{ Thos. Drue, c.
{ Phebe Dumont, c.
{ John Nevius, c.
{   and wife, c.
Jacob Probasco,
Phamatie Ditmars,
Peter Staats,
Maria Frelinghuysen,
{ Peter Voorhees,
{ Cath. Skilman,
Maria Van Ortwick,
  w. of Peter Stryker,
John Bainbridge,
Jacobus Garretson,
Martin Schenck.

Oct., 1798. Ab. F. Ditmars,
Martha Vechte,
  w. of Jacobus Garretson, Jr.
May, 1799. Peter Stryker, M. D.,
Maty Ditmars,
  wid. of Derick Hoagland.
July, 1799. Isaac Lott,
Helena Schenck,
  w. of Dr. Peter Stryker,
Gertje Rynierson,
Judith Beduyn,
  wid. of Sam. Williams.
April, 1800. John Staats, Jr.
Oct., 1800. Caty Blaw,
{ John Staats, c.
{ Charity Quick.
April, 1801. Cath. Van Matie,
  w. of Henry Didsbury,
Tone,
  slave of Rynier Smock.
Oct., 1801. John Zutphen,
Altye Wykoff,
  w. of Josiah Schenck,
Susanna Staats,
Mary Vechta,
  w. of John Staats,
Jane Rice, b.

Thomas,
  slave of Peter Wyckoff, b.
Maria Perrine,
  wid. of John Hardenbergh.
July, 1803. { Jacobus Van Nuys, c.
          { Mary Hoagland, c.
Nell, c.
Sarah Prall,
  w. of Dan. Hoagland.
April, 1805. Wm. Thompson,
Stephen Garretson,
Anne Middlesworth,
  w. of Isaac Lott.
Sept. Anne Hendrickson,
  w. of Gar. Terhune.
Nov. { Ab. Whitenegt,
     { Geertje Van Nuys,
Hannah,
  slave of Peter VanDoren, b.
Oct., 1807. Annetta Van Harlingen,
  wid. of Paul Duryea,
Eleanor McCollum,
  w. of Rynear Van Tyne, c.
Williampje Van Arsdalen,
  w. of Geo. Vroom.
Oct. Altie Terhune,
  w. of John Sutphen,
{ John M. Bayard, c.
{ Marg. Bayard, c.
May, 1808. Peter Kinney, c.
Ab. Staats, c.
Gitty Lott,
  w. of John Broach, c.
{ Johannes Ditmars, c.
{ Marg. Whitenack, c.
Oct. Hendrick Wilson,
Marg. Conover,
  w. of Coert Garretson.
May, 1809. { Farrington Barcaloo,
       { Hannah Bennett,
{ Peter Garretson,
{ Elizb. Polhemus,
Urias Van Cleef,
Henrietta Van Sinderin,
  w. of Martin Schenck,
Maria Van Duyn,
  w. of Peter Stryker.

John Frelinghuysen,
Leah Van Doren,
  w. of Wm. Van Doren, c.
Mrs. Mary Cooper, c.
Oct., 1809. Stintie Blaw,
    w. of —— Fisher,
Elizb. Schenck,
  w. of Hend. Staats,
Magdalen Staats,
  w. of John Vanderveer,
Sarah Wyckoff,
April, 1814. Elijah Hodge,
Cath. Van Zandt, w.
  of Adam Smith.
Cath. Smith, wid. of John
  Stryker.
Nelly Bennett, w. of Rich.
  Garretson.
Maria Van Doren, w. of
  Doctor Vredenburgh.
Mary Young.
Oct., 1814. Wm. McDowell.
Ann Brokaw, w. of John
  Stryker.
Dinah and Nancy, slaves of
  Eldert Smith.
James, slave of Isaac
  Stryker.
May, 1815. Mary Van Liew, w. of John
  Christopher.
  { Ab. Beekman, c.
  { Matilda Nevius,* c.
Maria Staats.
Oct., 1815. Elizabeth Roberts, w. of
  Uriah Van Cleef, b.
Mary French, w. of Mile
  Root.
John I. Stryker.
Bett, slave of Rev. J. L.
  Zabriskie, b.
Mile Root, c.
  { Roeloff Terhune, c.
  { Maria Ditmarse, c.
  { Jas. Van Pelt, c.
  { Sarah Todd, c.
Mary Nevins, w. of Cor.
  Cooper. c.

May, 1816. Elizabeth Edgar, w. of Peter
  Van Cleef, c.
Maria Broach, w. of Sam.
  Thomas.
Cath. Sebring, w. of Ab.
  Van Nest.
Anny Van Clief,* w. of Jas.
  Hagaman.
Mary Bergen, w. of Ab.
  Staats.
Getty Staats, w. of John
  Ditmars.
Nov., 1816. Wm. W. Perrine, Jr., c.
  { Nic. Bainbridge,
  { Ann Cornell.
Mary Van Cleef, w. of Isaac
  Van Cleef.
Cor. Van Huys.
Nelly Lott.*
Nelly Schenck.
Phebe Ann Garretson.
Jane Verbryck.
Nelly Broach.
May, 1817. Isaac Van Cleef.
Ab. Davis.
Gershom Burnhart.*
Cor. Broach.
John Van Doren.
Jane Merrill.
Laura Garretson, w. of Cor.
  Staats.
Johannah Bainbridge.
Nelly Smock.
Mary Thomas.
Pheby Lott.
  { Henry Stryker,
  { Laura Thompson.
Joseph, slave of Mr. Quick.
Ellen, w. of Jacob Bergen, c.
Gideon Hendrickson, c.
Nov., 1817. Cor. Van Sickle.
Lucretia Voorhees, w. of
  Ab. Brokaw.
Jane Van Doren.
Phebe Broach.
  { John M. Wyckoff,*
  { Maria Voorhees.

Wm. Wilson,
Jane Bergen.
Ab. Voorhees.
Johannth Sutphen. .... Apr., 1820.
Elizb. Bainbridge. ...... Oct., 1820.
Margaret Schureman, w. of
David Nevius, Jr., c.
Getty Voorhees, w. of Gerrit
Quick, c.
Martha Vechte, wid. of Jas.
Gerretson, c.
Maria Stryker.
Jemima Lubator, wid. of
John Van Nostrand.
May, 1818. Edward Van Harlingen.
Ab. Wyckoff.
Isaac Van Nuyse,
Sarah Staats.
Phebe Staats.
Henry Staats.
Abm. —————.
Bett, slave of Wm. Wyckoff, b.
Oct., 1818. Elizb. Williamson, w. of
Gideon Hendrickson.
Martha Van Nuys, w. of Ed
Van Harlingen.
Jane Tyson, wid. of Ab. P
Staats.
Marg. Terhune.
Susanna Nevius, w. of Douw
Ditmars.
Bradly Williams.
Mary Cushan, w. of John
Ditmars.
Jane, servant of Ed. Van
Harlingen.
Apr., 1819. Clemens Shepherd, w. of
Jos. Christopher.
Fred. King, c.
Abigail Laine, c.
John Stryker, c.
Ann Brokaw, c.
Oct., 1819. Sam. Van Doren, c.
Cath. Lucy Broach, w.
of Cor. Broach, c.
Cath. Voorhees, w. of Peter
P. Staats.

A. Van Doren, w. of Wm.
Voorhees.
Jane, slave of Peter Staats, b.
Elizb. Reed.
Fred. Frelinghuysen.
John Wilson.
Joseph Christopher.
Phebe Hoagland, w. of Martin Van Cleef.
Sarah Spader, w. of Jer.
Stryker.
Dick, slave of John Sutphen, b.
Isabel Wyckoff, w. of Ab.
Wyckoff, c.
Maria Van Nest, c.
Apr., 1821. Ann Schenck, w. of Corn.
Covenhoven.
John Van Zandt,
Elizb. Smith.
Jane Dumont, w. of Fred.
Frelinghuysen.
Elizb. Frelinghuysen, w. of
Jas. Elmendorf, M.D.
Cath. Williams, w. of Peter
Enlich.
Susan Little, w. of John Mitchell, b.
Mary L. Finley, w. of John
R. Davison, c.
Oct., 1821. Ann Baker, w. of John Waters.
Marg. Van Arsdalen, w. of
Peter Cortelyou.
John V. Gerritson.
Mary Lott, c.
Maria Van Nostrand, w. of
Isaac Hoff, c.
May, 1822. Elizb. Duryea.
Lydia Stryker, w. of Wm.
Cornell.
Jane Van Middleswort, w. of
Joachim Quick, c.
Oct., 1822. Wm. Blackwell,
Cath. Croeser.
Jacob Van Cleef,
Elizb. Gray.

Polly Bainbridge, w. of Nathaniel Plutin.

Rebecca Flagg, w. of Peter Smith.

Cath. Brokaw, w. of Isaac Van Arsdalen.

Jane Ann Duryea,* w. of John Van Cleef.

Eliz.Flagg,wid.ofJ.VanBrunt

Elizb. Duryea.

Lydia Stryker.

Jacob Schenck.

Cor. Covenhoven.

Wm. Cornell.

Hannah Wyckoff, w. of John Wilson.

Stephen Garretson, c.

Maria Thompson, c.

Elizb. ———, w. of ——— Voorhees, c.

Mary Ann Schenck.

Ellen Thompson.

Josiah Finley.

Douw Wilson.

Cyrenius Thompson.

Gerrit Garretson.

John Vanderveer.

Rynier Van Tyne.

Apr., 1823. { John V. M. Wyckoff, Ann Walters, b.

Abiah Enlich.

Rachel Monday, w. of David Collins,

Elizb. French, w. of Chris. Van Nostrand.

Ann Brokaw.

Elizb. Vliet.

Peter L. Sebring.

Mary Hagaman, b.

Cath. Smith,* w. of Wm. Hoagland.

Ann Mayhem, w. of Ab. Sardam, c.

Oct., 1823. { Isaac V. C. Stryker, Charity Voorhees.

Getty Van Pelt, w. of John Wyckoff.

Maria Wyckoff, w. of John Eich.

Dinah, slave of John Ditmars, b.

Sarah V. Middlesworth,* w. of Josiah Schenck,

Apr., 1824. Jane Wilson,* w. of Rynier Merrill.

Mary Brokaw, w. of Cor. Hoagland.

Almy W. Robinson, w. of Wm. T. Rogers.

Ann Brokaw, w. of Jacob Schenck.

Peter Kinnee.

Oct., 1824. { Nich. Bainbridge, c. Ann ———, c.

Cath. Van Nest, w. of Peter Sebring, c.

Dinah Suydam, wid.of Garret Van Cleef.

A—— Van Arsdalen, w. of Dan. Enlich.

Oct., 1825. Henry Wilson.

Apr., 1826. Josiah Schenck.*

Magdalen F. Stryker, w. of Peter Van Zandt.

Cath. Van Doren, w. of Simeon Van Nortwick.

Ann Coevert, w. of Cyrenius Thompson.

Nelly Freeland, w. of Aaron Hill, c.

Oct., 1826. James G. Quick.

Nelly Van Tyne.

{ Christopher Hoagland, c. Phebe Staats,* c.

May, 1827. Jemima Barcaloo, w. of John King, c.

Fred. F. Cornell.

Marg. Cornell, c.

Ann Maria Cornell, c.

Cath. Cornell, c.

Catalina Schenck, w. of Sam. M. Quick.

Leah M. Vleet, w. of James Quick.

John Wyckoff.

Oct., 1827. Jonathan Bennett.

Cor. Cornell, c.

Elizb. Bainbridge, w. of Wm. Wyckoff, c.

1828. CHURCH REBUILT.

May, 1829. Ann Stryker, w. of Peter ———.

John S. Stryker.

Douw J. Ditmars.

Deborah Vanderipe, w. of John Flagg, c.

Peter ———, c.

Sarah Kinsey, w. of David . Lewis, c.

Ellen Thomson, c.

Jonathan Smith, c.

{ Peter L. Suydam, c.
{ Maria Oakey, c.

Oct., 1829. Marg. Hageman, w. of Jas. Vanderveer.

Dinah Van Doren, w. of Jos. Voorhees. c.

May, 1830. Cor. Staats.

——— Stryker, c.

Oct., 1830. Maria Van Nostrand, w. of Jacob Smith.

Letty Van Doren, w. of Dennis Van Duyn.

{ Ab. Gerritson, c.
{ Elizabeth ———, c.

Apr., 1831. Ann Bennett, w. of John Probasco.

Thom., slave of John Wyckoff.

Rachel Collins, c.

Sarah Schenck, w. of Jos.. Van Doren, c.

Elizabeth Gibson, w. of Dan Brown, c.

Margaret, slave of Jacobus Quick, c.

Oct., 1831, { Rynier Staats,
{ Cath. Voorhees.
{ John Auten,
{ Cornelia Probasco.

Fred. Probasco.

Mariah Probasco.

{ Dan. Lewis,
{ Jane Ann Stryker.

James Van Nuys.

Peter Cornell.

Isaac Cornell.

Ellen Cornell.

Letty Cornell.

Dorothy Staats.

Ann S. Quick.

Sarah Cash.

Maria Flagg.

Sarah Suydam.

Mary Suydam.*

Mary Ann Wyckoff.*

Cornelia Ann Gerritson.

Elizabeth Hoagland.*

Magdalen Hoagland.

Elizabeth Harris, wid. of Peter Van Doren.

Mary Ann Skillman, widow of Jacob Stryker.

John W. Suydam.

Maria Suydam.

Maria Barcaloo. -

Hannah Barcaloo.

Maria Walter.

Susan Vanderveer.

Garret Wyckoff.

Maria Wyckoff.

Rachel Wyckoff.

Marg. Van Nostrand.

{ John Smock.*
{ Jane Mouday.

{ John A. Smith.*
{ Sarah Anten.

{ Cortlandt Voorhees,
{ Jane Ann Stryker.

Maria Van Cleef, w. of John Stryker.

Maria Stryker.

Peter J. Smith.

Susan Smith,

Cath. V. N. Smith.

Joseph Van Doren.

Sophia Ann Van Doren.

Margaret Ditmars, w. of Dr. McKissack.

John Van Liew,
Julian Sansbury
Adam Smith.
Jane Smith.*
Abigail Smith.*
Magdalen Van Zandt, w. of
Benj. Van Nostrand.
Jane Voorhees, w. of Wm
Smith.
Wm. T. Rodgers.
Stout McMachin,
Sarah Low.
Perrine Gerritson.
Jas. Perrine.
Henry Stryker,
Henry Bennett.
Isaac Bennet.
Priscilla Waters, w. of Peter
Lewis.
Peter Stryker,
Elsie Christopher.
Peter I. Nevius,*
Jane Vanderveer.*
Schenck Vanderveer,
Johannah Gerritson.
John Williamson.
Peter S. Williamson.*
Peter N. Beekman,*
John I. Van Cleef.
Cor. S. Nevius.
Ann Stryker.
Eleanor Stryker.
Martha Mumford.
Peter Smith.
Cath. Ann Smith.
Peter Staats.
Cath. Van Nostrand.
Nelly Van Nuys, w. of Stephen Gerritson.
Eleanor Gerritson.
Jane Ann Hageman.
Elizb. Stryker,* w. of Ab.
Polhemus.
Cornelia Polhemus.
Eliza Maria Thompson.
Letty Christopher.

Dorcas Stryker, w. of Ab.
Van Doren.
Matilda Van Liew, w. of Dan.
Disborough.
Cath. Quick.
Jane Wilson.*
John. J. Van Nostrand.
Peter P. Staats.*
John P. Staats.*
Johanna Van Doren.*
Ernestus Schenck.
Ann Skillman.*
Frank, slave of John Van
Doren.
Tite, slave of John Van
Doren.
Jane, slave of John P. Staats.
Rachel, slave of Rynier
Staats.
Nelly, slave of —— Van
Cleef.
Peggy, free wife of Thompson.
May, 1832. Nelly Greendike, w. of Henry
Wilson,
Maria, Wunpit,* w. of Peter
Cornell,
Cath. Wilson,* w. of Peter
P. Staats,
Peter Staats,
Stephen Renan,
Jane, slave of widow Hageman,
John J. Van Nest, c.
Francis Smith, c.
Peter J. Van Nest, c.
Idah Van Liew, w. of Peter
B. Van Doren,
Ab. Quick,* c.
Oct., 1832. James Staats, c.
Aletta Van Nuys, c.
Ann ——, c.
—— Van Veghte, c.
John Sutphen,
Letty Staats,
Maria Van Nuys, w. of Isaac
Sebring,

Victor Delvan,
Maria Delvan,
Cornelia, w. of Peter Fine,
Jane, slave of widow Hage
man,
Peggy ——,
May, 1833. Nancy Davis, c.
Hannah Davis, c.
Sarah, servant of Nancy
Davis, c.
Sarah Nevius, w. of Peter
Enlich, c.
Cath. Stevens, w. of John
Pittegrew, c.
Sylvia Wyckoff, w. of Cor.
Nevius, c.
Wm. French,* c.
Cornelius ——, c.
Henry Little, b.
Isabella ——, b.
Dinah French, w. of
Isaac Van Cleef, c.
Oct., 1833. Margaret Van Nest,
Cor. Cornell, c.
Sarah Ann Hunt, c.
May, 1834. Bergen ——,
Sarah J. Bellis, w. of P. Van
Doren, c.
Ellen Van Liew, w. of J.
Smith, c.
Oct., 1834. James Compton,
John Compton.
Mary Coop, w. of Wm. Reed,
Peter A. Dumont, c.
Cath. Miner,* w. of Peter
Daly, c.
May, 1835. Rachel Van Liew, b.
Wm. Longe Taylor,
Peter D. Quick, c.
{ Ab. H. Brokaw,* c.
{ Gertrude Staa s, c.
Oct., 1835. Cor. Van Nest,
Gerrit Quick,
John Van Zandt,*
Johannah Bergen,
Mary Ann French, w. of·
Garret Van Liew, c.

Prudence Longstreet, w. of
Geo. Walber, c.
Idah Van Duyn, w. of Ed.
Van Harlingen, c.
Apr., 1836. Mary Ann Van Arsdale, w.
of Paul Lewis, b.
Susanna Staats, c.
Oct., 1836. Catharine, w. of John W.
Bush, c.
Peter Staats,
Jane Staats,
Garret Bergen,
Maria Bergen,
Phebe Bergen,
Adam Kipsey,
Phebe Staats,
Sarah Van Arsdalen, w. of
John Van Nostrand,
Rachel Van Zandt,
John Ditmars.
May, 1837. { John Van Doren Hoag-
{ land,* :
{ Magdalen Garretson,+
Ann Joanna Hulick,*
Jacob Wortman,
{ Henry Schenck, c.
{ Eliza Wilson, c.
Phebe Hix, w. of Jacob
Wortman, c.
Oct., 1837. Peter Polhemus,
Cornelia Polhemus,
Sarah Gerretson,
Magdalen Gerretson, w. of
Peter Smith,
Sarah Van Pelt, w. of Isaac
Van Cleef,
Ann Maria Voorhees,
Letitia Gernow,
{ Ralph T. Sutphen,*
{ —— French,
Sarah ——.
{ Henry Staats,
{ Helen Staats,
L. Staats,
w. of —— ——,
Elizabeth Whitenech,*
w. of John I. Staats,

Henry Hulick,
John W. Bush, c.
{ Cornelia Low, c.
{ Sarah Van Duyn, c.
John J Staats, c.
Edward Thompson, c.
May, 1838. { Cor. P. Brokaw,
{ Catharine ——,
Susan V. Kemp,
{ Alfred French,
{ Eliza Silvis, b.
Mary Hoagland,
w. of Jas. Hultz,
Isaac L. Van Cleef,
Ab. Suydam,*
Wm. J. Thompson,
Peter A. Polhemus,
{ Wm. Sunderland, c.
{ Leah Powelson, c.
{ Henry Powelson,* c.
{ Lydia Stryker,* c.
{ Dan. Lewis, c.
{ Jane Stryker, c.
{ John W. Quick, c.
{ Sarah Stryker,
Peter Wortman, c.
John Breeze, c.
Bergen H. Van Vliet, c.
Maria N. ——ster,
w. of John Taylor, c.
Oct., 1838. Rebecca Van Kemp,
w. of Fred. Ten Eyck,
John J. Ditmars,*
Sarah Cornell,
James Burnhart, †
{ Priam Staats,
{ Dian
May, 1839. Elizabeth Peterson,*
w. of John Van Zandt, c.
Oct., 1839. Mary Ann Gulick,
w. of Cor. Wooley,
Diana, belonging to
Wid. C. Voorhees,
Betty,
belonging to Ab. Quick.

May, 1840. Peter Daily, b.
Cor. S. Hoagland, c.
Mary T. Elvira, c.
C. Wilson, c.
Oct., 1840. { Garret Quick, c.
{ Adaline Voorhees, c.
{ Henry Bl——, c.
{ Sarah J. Voorhees, c.
{ John G. Voorhees, c.
{ Eliza Voorhees, c.
Eliza W—d—r,
w. of Peter Wortman.
Oct., 1841. John Rynierson, b.
Marg. Miner, c.
{ Jas. L. Voorhees,* c.
{ Maria Smith,* c.
Maria Van Arsdalen,
w. of Peter J. Van Nest, c.
Maria Pieter,
w. of Wm. Vroom, c.
Ann Vroom, c.
May, 1842. Dinah Van Cleef,
Selah Woodhull,
Cath. Van Nuys,
w. of Isaac Lott,
Sarah Street,
w. of John Sauls,
Ann Dumont,
wid. of Jas. Voorhees,
Ann Porter,
w of Ab. Vroom,
Gertrude Broach.
Oct., 1842. Isaac Lott,
Henrietta Broach,
Ann,
slave of —— ——,
Eliza ——,
w. of Peter ——.
May, 1843. Peter Lewis,
Rachel Johnson,
w. of John Bellis,
Rebecca Bellis,
Marg. McKissack,*
Sarah Elmendorf,
w. of Dr. Elmendorf,

† Now Rev. Jas. Bernart, of Boardville.

{ John Van Doren,*
{ Charity Staats,*
{ John Smith,
{ Elizb. Ann Van Zandt,
Matilda Nevius,
Ann Lott,
{ Benj. Smith,
{ Ann Brokaw,*
{ Peter Stryker,
{ Elsie Christopher
{ Peter Sullivan,
{ Sarah Snyder.

Oct., 1843. Marg. Annin,
Cath. Burnhart,
Ellen Thomas,
Cath. Disborough,
Henry Coleman,
John Broach,
Elizb. Ann Van Cleef,
    wid. of Peter Polhemus,
Eliza Ann Polhemus,
    w. of Herman Dilty.

May, 1844. { And. Vroom,
{ Maria Ditmars,
{ Roeloff T. Ditmars,*
{ Sarah Brokaw,
Mary Ann Staats,
    w. of Adrian Merrill,
Joachim Quick,
Mary A. Zabriskie,
{ Henry Hulick, c.
{ Alliebah Jane Stillwell, c.
Maria Stryker,
    w. of John Fine, c.

Oct., 1844. Isaac W. Van Doren,
Phebe Van Duyn,
    w. of Peter Wyckoff, c.
Titus Wnyphey, c.
{ Hannibal Nevius, c.
{ Hagar, c.

May, 1845. Mary Van Cleef,
Christian Bodinot,
    w. of Joseph H. Stryker, c.
{ Isaac Cornell, c.
{ Maria Flagg, c.
Deborah Vanderipe,
    w. of John Flagg, c.

Ellen Cornell, c.
Cath. Broach,
    wid. of David Gulick, c.
Nancy Gulick, c.
Elizb. Ann Hoagland,
    w. of Wm. Wyckoff, c.
Elizb. Hephun,
    w. of Jac. Suydam, c.
Phebe Staats,*
    w. of Ab. Voorhees, c.
Mary Van Vliet.

Oct., 1845. Tunis Freener,
    w. of Wm. ———.

May, 1846. Isaac Van Cleef,
Mary Van Cleef,*
    w. of Staats Van Nuys,
Ab. Van Nest,
Prime Ditmars.

Oct., 1846. Peter Bergen,
Elizb. Peterson,
Rachel Ann Smith,*
    w. of Ab. Van Nest,
Maria Hagaman,
    w. of Wm. Ann Duyn,
Dinah Ten Eyck,
    w. of John Francis Cl—.

May, 1847. John C. Rosecrantz,
Wm. Wyckoff,
Maria Brokaw,*
    w. of John R. Staats,
Maria Cortelyou,
    w. of Peter Wortman, c.

Oct., 1847. Thomas Staats, c.

April, 1848. John B. Smith,
Susanna Gerno,*
{ Peter Daily, c.
{ Cath. Miner,* c.

Oct., 1848. Peter V. D. Broach,
Cath. Stryker,
{ Peter Dumont Voorhees, c
{ Marg. A. Sutphen, c.
{ Cor. Messler, c.
{ Anna Wyckoff, c
{ Cor. J. Gulick,*
{ Sarah Ann Voorhees, c.
{ Hannibal Nevius, c.
{ Hagar, c.

May, 1849. Leah Adaline Van Doren,
  w. of Henry Coleman, b
  Gertrude Schenck,
  w. of Ab. Davis,
  Cath. Davis,
  Mary Voorhees,*
  { Ab. Veghte,*
  { Ann Van Nest,*
  Jane Van Nuys,
  w. of Brogun Van Nuys,
  Jane Ann Stryker,
  wid. of Court Voorhees.
Oct., 1849. Maria Vroom, b.
  Idah Jane ——,
  w. of Caleb Brokaw,
  Elizb. Gerno,*
  Peter S. Hoagland,
  Jane A. De G——,
  w. of —— Van Doren, c.
  Mary ——,
  w. of Josiah Davis, c.
May, 1850. Jane Van Doren,
  w. of James Costiton,
  Mary Schenck,
  Cath. Ann Van Doren,
  Ann Y. Elmendorf,*
  John V. A. Merrill,
  Catharine Thompson, c.
  Mary Powelson,
  wid. of John Hoagland, c.
  Ann Thompson,*
  w. of Arthur Quick, c.
  Mary Cox, wife of
  John Isaac Voorhees, c.
  Jane Voorhees, c.
  Mary Voorhees, c.
Oct., 1850. Peter Q. Voorhees,*
  Esther Ann Wyckoff,
  Mary Elizb. Voorhees,
  Ida Nevius,*
  w. of Reuben H. Hulick,
  Ab. J. Voorhees,
  Dr. James B. Elmendorf,
  Eliza Merrill,
  wid. of Cor. Van Nuys,
  Mary Polhemus,
  w. of John Steins,

Sarah Ann Snyder,
  w. of Ab. H. Brokaw,
  Charlotte L. Gillette,
  w. of Rev. John DeWitt,c.
May, 1851. Wm. H. Van Doren,
  Henry Schenck,
  Cath. Maria Gulick,
  w. of John Gerno,
  Adaline Hoagland,
  w. of Jas. Garretson, c.
  { James G. Voorhees,* c.
  { Jane Skillman,* c.
  Ellen Schenck,*
  w. of Dan. Disborough, c
  Sarah Van Arsdale,
  wid. of Jas. Voorhees,
  Sarah Voorhees,
  Aletta Voorhees,
  Jane Voorhees.
Oct., 1851. { Peter S. Vanderveer,*
  { Sarah Everet,*
  { Peter C. Staats,*
  { Magdalen Gerno,*
  { John Henry Wilson,*
  { Mary Jane Howell,*
  Sarah D. Howell,
  Adaline Van Cleef,
  Maria S. Powelson,
  Jane Powelson,
  w. of Ed. Christopher,
  John V. D. Nevius,
  Maria L. Nevius,*
  Susanna V. Nevius,*
  Elizabeth Smith,*
  w. of Peter P. Stryker,
  Jacob Gulick,
  Adrian Merrill,
  { Wm. Hulse,*
  { Elizb. W. Hoagland,*
  Jane D. Van Cleef,*
  Elizb. E. Bernhart,*
  Cath. Jane French,
  Martha Maria French,*
  Caleb Brokaw,
  Cath. Smith,
  wid. of Jas. Frederick,
  John Steins,

Anna Kirkpatrick,
   w. of Henry Schenck, c
{ Isaac Gulick, o.
{ Syche DeHart, c.
Cornelia Van Zandt,*
   w. of Isaac Sebring, c
Aletta J. Van Arsdale,*
   w. of Wm. M. K. Smith, c.
Feb., 1852. Jas. Garretson,
Peter S. Ditmars,*
Jonathan W. Wilson,*
Jacob J. Garretson,*
Richard F. French,
Getty Stultz,
   wid. of Wm. W Pierson,
Charlotte Maria Broach,
Cath. M. Van Doren,
   wid. of Cor. S. **Hoagland,**
Maria Wyckoff,
   w. of Wm. H. Van Doren,
Cath. Van Alst,
   wid. of Joshua Martin,
Adaline Van Cleef,
Jane Van Veste,
Wm. M. K. Smith,*
Jane Polhemus,
Ellen V. N. Garretson,
   d. of Perrine G.,
Silas DeWitt,
Matilda Van Nuys,* c.
June, 1725. Adeline Voorhees,*
   w. of Isaac A. **Van Cleef,**
Sarah Wilson,
Catharine Sebring,*
Elizabeth Davis,
Maria Merrill,*
Frank Polhemus,
{ **John D.** Van Nuys, **c.**
{ Matilda B. Voorhees, c.
Sarah Garretson,*
   w. of Benj. C. Smith, c.
Maria Flagg,*
   w. of Cor. H. Broach, c.
Oct., 1852. Rachel Matilda Wyckoff,
Elizabeth Elmendorf,
Diana Terhune,

Geo. Labagh,
Judy Robinson,
Cor. Cornell, c.
Feb., 1853. Wm. Rynnerson, b.
Cath. Van Nostrand,
Cath. Jane Smith,*
Sarah Staats,
   w. of J. J. Garretson,
Wm. Voorhees, c.
June, 1853. Anna S. Garretson,*
   w. of Selah W. Smith,
Helen Ann Van Doren,
   w. of Rich. H. Kuhl,
Hannah Hopkins,
Rich. H. Kuhl, c.
Mrs. Ann Probasco, c.
Ellen Wyckoff,
   w. of Isaac Garretson, c.
Ellen **Van Tyne,*** c.
Oct., 1853. Maria V. Ditmars,
Anna E. Ditmars,*
Cath. Ann Sutphen,*
Matilda Beekman,
   w. of Dr. L. H. Mosher, c.
Cath. Onderdonk,
   w. of John B. Wyckoff, c
Feb., 1854. John Sutphen,
Cath. Beekman,
   w. of Jac. W. Beekman.
June, 1855. **Gertrude Fisher,**
   w. of Wm. **Abbott,**
Lydia Ann Gillette,
Ellen Louisa Broach,
Hannah Marg. Van Nostrand,
   w. of Dan. Hutchinson, c.
Oct., 1855. **Gertrude** Staats,*
   w. of Cor. J. Lane,
Helen Jane Merseroll, w. of
   Wm. Harris Van Doren,
Maurice V. Laurens,
Peter L. Powelson, c.
Joseph Kennedy, b.,
Theodosia Wyckoff,*
Joanna Nevins.
Feb., 1856. Hannah Elizb. **Redding,**
Cor. J. Lane, c.

June, 1856. Jacob Theodore Wyckoff,
    { Henry V. Stryker,
    { Sarah Elizb. Van Nuys,
    Cath. E. Stryker,
       ᵔ w. of Josiah J. Schenck,
    Gertrude Brokaw,
    Gertrude Powelson,
    Martha Sebring,
    { Harry Nevius,*
    { Henrietta,*
    Diana,
       servt.of Josiah Schenck,b
    { John Vred. Van Neste,* c
    { Mary Tabitha Stryker,* c
    Adaline Stryker,*
       w. of D. S. Young, c.
Oct., 1856. Marg. Beardslee,* b.
    Rachel Beardslee,*
       w. of P. N. Beekman, b.
    Jane M. Huff,
       w. of John S. Wyckoff, c.
    Mary Dolliver,
       w. of Alex. B. Staats, c.
    Cath. Van Vleck, c.
    Cath. M. Suydam,* c.
    Mary Voorhees,*
       w. of Cor. Gulick, o.
    Phebe Staats,*
       w. of C. L. Hoagland, c.
    Gertrude Hoagland.
May, 1857. Isaac Sebring, Jr.,*
    Sarah Maria Van Vleck,
    Ellen Ann Hoagland,
    Mary Walyns, w. of Joseph
       Phillips, c.
    Sarah Maria Hoagland,* w
       of John Vande Ripe, c.
Sept., 1857. Maria Voorhees, widow of
    —— Cornell, c.
    { David C. Hubbard,*
    { Mary ——,* c.
    Martha Hummer,* w. of P.
       S. Williamson.
Mar., 1858. Ab. V. D. Staats,*
    Sarah H. Bernart,*
    Mary Elizb. Van Doren,
    Francis Van Vleck,

    Marg. Ann Nevius,
    Margaret Powelson, w. of
       Peter L. Powelson, c.
Jun., 1858. { Caleb Brokaw, Jr.,
       { Mary Eliz. Veghte,
    John VanderRipe,*
    Matilda R. Merrill,*
    { Cor. G. Van Cleef,
    { Maria G. Hoagland,
    Sarah Maria Gulick,
    Jane Ann Garretson,*
    Henrietta Brokaw,* w. of H.
    ᵔ V. D. Stryker,
    { Jas. J. Garretson, c.
    { Elsie Wortman,*
    Mary Voorhees,* w. of Min-
       na V. Van Doren, c.
    Jas. H. Stryker, c.
    Elizb. Stryker, wid. of Ab.
       Stryker,
    Abby Ann Sater.
Sep., 1858. { John C. Van Vliet,
       { Mary Merrill,
    { James Van Nuys,*
    { Letitia Staats,*
    { Isaac V. C. Wyckoff,*
    { Cath. Wyckoff,*
    Henry S. Van Nuys,*
    Harriet Beardslee,
    Cath. Blackwell,*
    Eleanor French,*
    Jane Ann Cornell,*
    Theresa Van Cleef,
    Abigail V. Gulick,*
    Alette Jane Stryker,*
    Mrs. Patience Rockfellow,
    Sarah Staats,* w. of Henry S.
       Van Nuys, c.
    Jane Staats, wid. of James
       J.Stryker.
Feb., 1859. John Staats,*
    Virginia Schenck,
    John Shields Haynes,* b.
    { Elijah Ronser, c.
    { Maria Bergen, c.
May, 1859. Fred. A. Smith,*
    Mary Ann Polhemus,* w. of

Law. V. Van Nuys,
Mary Elmerdorf,*
{ Sam. Francis,* b.
{ Jane Ann Van Doren,* c.
{ Sanford B. Wakeman,* c.
{ Cath. Van Vliet,* c.
{ John B. Wykoff, c.
{ Cath. Onderdonk, c.
Jas. Nevius,* c.
Oct., 1857. Henry Wilson,
Cath. A. Hoagland,
Holloway W. Pierce, c.
Lydia Voorhees,* w. of Josiah S. Smith, c.
Feb., 1860. James H. Hageman,*
Mary Gertrude Sutphen,*
Lucinda Skinner. w. of Isaac Hughey.
June, 1860. Lydia A. Powelson,*
John Garretson,†
{ Whilden Foster, b.
{ Jane O. Baker, b.
Maria H. Hulce,*
Elizb. Stryker,* w. of Thos...
Layton,
Christina Flagg,* c.
Mrs. Maria Sylvester, c.
Jas. H. Sylvester, c.
{ Abraham Quick,* c.
{ Martha French,* c.
Oct., 1860. Mary A. Voorhees,*
Sarah Wyckoff,* wid. of Jac. Smith, c.
Letty Flagg, w. of Wm. F.
Feb., 1861. Alex. B. Staats,*
Cornelia A. Stryker,*
Sarah S. Stryker,
Mary Voorhees,*
Ab. Davis, c.
Lemmy Cordelia Hulick,*
Josephine Outhout Van Harlingen,
Martha Louisa Annen,
{ Ralph Voorhees, c.
{ Ann B. Brokaw, c.
June, 1861. Jacob V. N. Smith,*
†Now a licentiate.

Peter W. Garretson,*
{ Car. V. N. Field,*
{ Josiah Boisnot,* c.
{ Elizabeth Stryker,* c.
Phebe Smith,* w. of John Cruser, c.
Oct., 1861. { Joseph Christopher,*
{ Cath. M. Van Nuys,*
Anna Maria Merrill,*
Anna Maria Ditmars,*
Charlotte S. DeWitt,
John W. French,
Magdalena VanderRipe,
Maria Louisa Smith,*
Gertrude Wilson,* w. of Wm. Blackwell,
Ann Lott, w. of Isaac Davis,
Jane Ann Houghton, w. of John Rightmire, c.
Feb., 1862. James Y. Elmendorf,*
John R. Ditmars,*
Dinah V. C. French,*
{ Peter W. Wikoff,* c.
{ Cath. A. Ditmars,* c.
June, 1862. Cor. Elizb. Smith,*
Marg. V. D. Lott, w. of Peter Powelson, c.
Henry Hulick, c.
{ Joseph Conover,* c.
{ Jane Hoagland,* c.
Mary E. Conover,* c.
Sep., 1862. Ellen Ann Conover,*
Feb., 1863. Matilda Beekman,*
Fannie M. Beekman,*
Sarah G. Van Nest,*
Cath. Van Nest,
Cath. S. Hoagland,
Sarah Van Doren, w. of Jack Van Doren.
May, 1863. Martha L. Brokaw,*
Cath. J. A. Brokaw,*
Henry P. Hoagland,*
Henrietta Holmes,
{ Alex. B. Brokaw, c.
{ Letitia Quick, c.
Thos. Hobart,* c.
Sarah H. Hobart,* c.

{ John H. Vandervoort,* c.
{ Eliza Brokaw,* c.
Elizb. H. Vandervoort,* c.
Aletta Ann Vandervoort,* c.
Mary S. Vandervoort,* c.
Oct., 1863. Sarah Aletta Staats,*
Feb., 1864. Mary E. Brokaw,*
Maria Stryker,*
Mary Esther Kipp,* w. of
Rev. E. T. Corwin, c.
May, 1864. Cor. H. Broach,*
Elizb. S. Merrill,*
Eleanor Schenck,* w. of
Sam. Brown, c.
Sarah Jane Voorhees,*
Sarah Auten,
Sarah E. VanNostrand,* w.
of Jacob V. N. Smith, c.
{ Wm. C. Burniston, c.
{ Jane Ann Cornell, c.
Anna Wyckoff,* c.
Aug., 1864. Martha V. Gulick,*
Martha Batcheller,* w. of
Jas. Y. Elmendorf, c.
Sar.Smith,* w.of J. Haynes.
Nov., 1864. { Israel Fisher,* c.
{ Maria Vanderipe,* c.
Sarah Staats, c.
Eleanor Smith,* w. of Gerard
Voorhees, c.
Maria S. French, wid. of
Ab. G. Van Nest, c.
Guretta Q. Powelson,* wid.
of Wm. Gulick, c.
Isaac W. Van Doren,* c.
Feb., 1865. Isaac H. Powelson,*
Ab. Van Cleef,*
Margaret Van Doren,*
Anna M. Van Deventer,*
Lewis H. Colthra,* c.
John Van Nest,*
May, 1865. Julia Miller,*
Cor. B. Veghte,*

Sarah V. N. Veghte,*
Alex. A. Brokaw.
{ Joseph H. Van Cleef,' c.
{ Mary Jane Field,* c.
Hannah F. Vroom, c.
Henry Hulick,* c.
{ Philip E. Van Arsdale,* c.
{ Elcy Voorhees,* c.
Cath. Skillman,* w. of Wm.
D. Van Dyke, c.
Lucy S. Van Dyke,* c.
Mary O. Servis,* w. of John
Hoagland, c.
Aug., 1865. Wm. G. Williamson,*
Sarah Jane Conover.
Susan Dinah Wyckoff,*
Mary Ann Felmly,* w. of
Ab. Van Cleef, c.
Ellen Van Nuys. c.
Nov., 1865. Magdalene Van Nuys.*
Sarah Jane Nevius,* w. of
Elias Wilson, c.
{ Wm. E. Mattison,*M.D.,c.
{ Frances T. Race.* c.
Feb., 1866. Caroline Staats.
May, 1866. Eliza T. Beekman,* wife of
Fred. V. L. Voorhees, c.
Mrs. Isabella Scott,*
{ Albert Voorhees,* c.
{ Kate Blackwell,* c.
Ann Eliza Jewell,* wid. of
Ab. Veghte,
Cath. Smith,* wife of James
Garretson, c.
Aug., 1866. Garret Voorhees.* c.
{ John I. Van Cleef,* c.
{ Eliza Van Doren,* c.
Ann Eliza Smith.*
Mary T. Van Nest,*
Mary Ann Apgar,* w. of
Zelius Culver,
Peter G. Quick.*

www.ingramcontent.com/pod-product-compliance
Lightning Source LLC
Chambersburg PA
CBHW030536270326
41927CB00008B/1406